My 90 Year Journey

Margaret Muirhead

ISBN: 978-1-925515-62-6

Published by Vivid Publishing
P.O. Box 948, Fremantle
Western Australia 6959
www.vividpublishing.com.au

Cover by Zoe Beatty, based on a woodcut by Sue Codee.

Cataloguing-in-Publication data is available from the National Library of Australia

CONTENTS

Section 4 – New Horizons

Section 5 – Finding Margaret

Section 6 – A Brief Retirement

Section 7 – And Then

SOMEONE SHOULD WRITE THE STORY OF...

Becoming a Grandmother.

Not just any old grandmother – not just an old woman who needs to be listened to, made a fuss of, needs to be included in family gatherings simply because 'she's still *there*'...

But a grandmother who has become a person of value in the lives of her grandchildren, and even of their friends – a person who is able to accept her young ones in whatever form they present themselves – tough, showing off, demanding, frank, even shocking, off-hand or affectionate.

This grandmother is still physically active, mentally available. She is not very tall. She has grey hair of course; wrinkled cheeks of course; glasses, hearing aids, supports in her shoes; even false teeth which she pretends are a secret. *This* grandmother has always had time to listen to any story that her grandchild wants to tell her, however long and obscure that story seems to be. She doesn't only half listen as she did to her own children...

She remembers those far off days when her daughter filled the kitchen with her complaints of the other girls at school "who are *so mean*", "who run off and hide", "who have better bikes than mine"... *That* mother, in those days, was still coming to terms with trying to be a good wife, a good housewife, a reasonable cook and a passable mother. She would sometimes seem to be not quite listening, seem to be more interested in the casserole she was preparing, or the baby who was messing up the cupboards, and would seem to say, "Mmm….?" or, "Oh, never mind…" more often than her daughter wanted to hear. Her attention was divided amongst a hundred other problems that were filling her day. Her daughter was not getting the rapt audience that she needed to restore her sense of fairness and well-being. That mother was not totally *there* for her poor daughter. The only thing they both really shared in those moments was a faint sense of failure!

Neither of them could imagine that forty years later this woman would focus *totally* on every word that any one of her grandchildren would be willing to say to her, and would have a supportive answer, and a reassuring word of praise if that was needed.

So how did this elderly woman discover the listening skill, the supportive attitudes, the gentle, non-judgemental advice that seems to keep her grandchildren, all nine of them, willing to share some of their closest moments with her, captivated by her spirit, by her enthusiasm and by her single-minded, unconditional, joyful and selfless love?

It has been a long journey that has brought a timid, nervous, shy child, through the startling years of adolescence, the demanding years of marriage and childbirth, and the steep learning curve of an unexpected work experience, to this mature, confident and surprisingly contented ninety year old woman.

* * *

This is where it all started. A simple writing exercise: '*Someone should write the story of……*'.

It was part of a five week writing workshop I attended several years ago.

I didn't know whether I could find the self discipline to recall the whole of all these nine decades.

But at last I have. And here it is.

I hope it is a story that you may find worth reading.

Margaret Muirhead

SECTION 1
THE BEGINNING

ARDOTTE ARRIVES

So… this story starts many years ago…

In 1926, on Friday 3rd December, a very small baby girl, with long black untidy hair, was born to Jean Craig Frayne in a suburban hospital in Adelaide, South Australia. This little dot was the fourth child of Jean and her husband, Harold Victor Frayne. Two boys, aged 9 and 7, and another girl, aged 3 had preceded her in this family. They had all recently moved from Balaklava, a dry, dusty farming town about 60 miles north of Adelaide, and settled into the fairly well-to-do seaside suburb of Glenelg.

The nurses in the hospital were fascinated by the little black-haired baby, and tied a huge pink bow around her straggly hair. They cooed over her as they brought her in to Jean, saying:

"Ah, Mrs Frayne, she's just a little dot!"

And so it happened that, although the fourth and youngest child of the Glenelg dentist and his wife was named Margaret Hamilton, she was, from that moment, called Ardotte by her family and their friends. As she grew a little bit more, her brothers called her 'George' for no particular reason that anyone could think of, and Ardotte and George were the names that were used most of the time in that household.

Ardotte remained a scrap of a girl, with big brown eyes and the thick black hair that she was born with. Her brothers, Bruce and Keith, towed her around in a box-cart that they had made, and her sister, Helen, tucked her into her doll's pram beside a couple of other dolls and wheeled her around the rather untidy garden that surrounded the brick bungalow in which they all lived. The boys went to the Glenelg State Primary School and Helen, when she turned five, was dressed in a brown uniform and, with yellow straw hat and brown gloves, went to Woodlands Girls' Grammar School.

Little Ardotte's early life proceeded fairly normally. On beach picnics, of which there were quite a few, her mother would dig a bit of a hole in the sand, put a beach towel over the damp hole and pop Ardotte into it for her afternoon nap. The boys would give her bone-rattling rides in their go-cart, mainly down the steep ramp into their dug-out in the backyard. And on one near fatal day, her father cranked up the old family car to drive back to work after lunch, and, hearing a bit of clinking under the chassis, bent down to check what was causing that bothersome rattle. He was alarmed to see the diminutive Ardotte under the car, happily lying on her tummy building little castles with the gravel and dirt of the driveway.

By 1929 the Great Depression was taking its toll of people's bank balances and their spending money, and Harold was finding that the dental practice that he shared with Frankie Smerdon in Glenelg was not bringing in quite enough patients, or quite enough pounds, shillings and pence to keep Harold's young family reasonably well fed. Jean had quite a good business head, and, although she had some serious doubts from a social standing point of view, she also had a pragmatic acknowledgement of the benefits of moving to a cheaper suburb. So she suggested that Harold should re-locate his practice, and his family, to the Main North Road near Prospect. This was the main artery into the city from the farming plains that spread to the north of Adelaide. Jean had lived all of her life in Balaklava (apart from her two final, 'finishing' school years at the Methodist Ladies' College in South Adelaide), and Harold had worked in Balaklava as the first resident dentist for 10 or more years. So it seemed reasonable to think that country friends and acquaintances from 'the old days', needing some work done on their teeth, would stop off at the home-based surgery at 159 Main North Road on their way into the city.

Unfortunately for Jean the address of her new home was not the good-sounding one of 'Prospect,' but the *rather common* sounding one of 'Nailsworth,' an immovable fact that she could never wholly accept. But the move was beneficial to Harold's practice, the rent of the slightly larger house was a little less than the rent they were receiving from the Glenelg bungalow, and the schooling opportunities were more acceptable, and affordable, than in the seaside suburb.

Moving the family of six from one suburb to another was a major exercise, and provided little Ardotte's first experience of terror. This skinny little three and a half year old girl with large brown eyes and long brown plaits was rather bewildered by all the commotion in the house as boxes and cases were packed and stacked. So she took refuge on the front veranda, waiting for all the turmoil to settle down.

Suddenly, through the heavy wooden front door, loomed two huge men struggling with her mother's enormous walnut piano and almost tripping over the small child squatting on the red cement step.

"Git outa the way, kid," roared one of these giants. "Go on, gitcha. Scram!!"

Little Ardotte scrambled to her feet, clutching the two peg-dolls she had been playing with. She scuttled across the un-mown front lawn and burrowed into the rough pine hedge that lined the front garden, making herself as invisible as possible. Fear and horror took hold of her.

It was much later that her brother was able to persuade her to come out of her hidey-hole and see that the chaos of her world was quietening down again.

That night, the final night in the Glenelg bungalow, asleep in the enclosed veranda that all four children slept in, Ardotte had a horrible dream. She dreamed that a very tall man with a weird animal's head kept walking back and forth past the wire screening of the lean-to sleep-out, occasionally growling quietly, waiting for her to wake up so he could take her away to some terrifying, unknown den.

These first memories stayed with her, and haunted her for the rest of her life.

NAILSWORTH

The house at 159 Main North Road was a bluestone and white limestone solid building with an intricately tiled return verandah at the front and a wide red cement verandah at the back. It had high ceilings, thick walls and a concrete underground cellar that half filled with water during the winter. It was bigger than the Glenelg bungalow, but as Harold's surgery and waiting room took up two of the front rooms of the house there was not enough space for all four children to sleep in the main part of the house. Ardotte and her sister, Helen, shared a room opposite the kitchen, and the two boys slept in a small lean-to asbestos clad sleep-out at the back.

The high ceilings, thick walls and a dark central passage kept the house cool in the fierce summers of Adelaide, and two fireplaces provided pockets of warmth in the winter. The only toilet, in those days called 'the lav,' was outside, down a vine covered trellis, past an ivy-covered rusty tank, and into a very small room with a wooden seated lavatory and a pull-chain for flushing.

'If you want a cool surprise,
Pull the chain before you rise,'

and a couple of other such ditties were scrawled on the walls by the boys. There was also a rather large tarantula spider, weirdly named 'Aloiscious', that used to lurk in the cob-webby corners of this little box room. The light for this important place was operated from within the house, so it was a great joke for one of the boys to switch off the light just as his sisters had made the scary dark trip through the tunnel of vines and ivy. Consequently a 'chamber pot' tucked under her bed was young Ardotte's preferred means of her nightly toilet management.

The house, inappropriately named 'Belle Vue,' looked out onto a noisy tram line on the busy Main North Road. Trucks from the Abattoir rumbled past through the day, and motor bikes roared along the road at all hours. It was not quite the peaceful atmosphere of the pleasant seaside suburb that the family had just left.

But the house was set on two large blocks of land. A wooden trellis of grape vines covered the northern and eastern sides of the house and various large fruit trees filled half of the garden space. The rest of the yard was covered in waist high grass, a couple of lawns and a large tin shed. As the world slid into the Great Depression of the 1930's Harold and the boys cleared large areas of this land and grew vegetables, created a chooks yard and built a rough stable for two horses and a cow.

For Jean, part farm girl, part aspiring city matron, this was perhaps a compromising base from which she could launch her children into Adelaide society. The greatest drawback for Jean was that unfortunate address—Main North Road *Nailsworth*, rather than the more respectable 'Prospect'. Worse, it was almost next door to the Nailsworth State School. (*Ugh*).

She was so disturbed by the 'Nailsworth' address that she insisted on using 'Prospect' as their mailing address, as well as in the telephone directory. Consequently, all letters were delivered to the Prospect Post Office—almost a mile away—rather than the Nailsworth Office, which was diagonally opposite to the house on Main North Road. This caused great inconvenience for the Postie who had to make a special trip up a steep hill to get to the family letter box which was almost hidden behind the shiny brass plate which announced 'Harold Frayne Dentist' and graced the low wooden front gate.

But in compensation for this unappealing address, the boys, Bruce and Keith, having done their time at a State school in Glenelg, were enrolled in the most prestigious Church of England Collegiate of Saint Peter's Boys' School, about four miles away. They rode their horses to school each day, as did various others of their friends. Helen, still in the brown uniform and yellow hat, finished her year at the Woodlands Girls' Grammar School, even though at the tender age of seven and a half she had to catch two trams each day to reach this equally prestigious school. Obviously, my Mother's ambitions for a foot-hold in Adelaide society were being fulfilled as she was able to persuade my Father to send his children to these fine private schools.

Ardotte, on her own for many hours of the day, played quietly in leafy corners of the garden. A massive mulberry tree and a cavernous hole in a big prickly bougainvillea bush provided private shelter for her and her much loved brown teddy-bear to create their own imaginary world. At times Tigger, the large ginger cat, a favourite of Harold's, would join her, especially for her private tea parties.

Harold carried on his dental practice in the front room of the house, seeing patients each morning, and also in the evening. In the afternoons he caught a tram into his practice on North Terrace in the City, where he shared rooms with his brother, Earnest, who was a doctor, (a definite step up in the social scale, which pleased Jean a lot).

At the Main North Road surgery, general anaesthetics were often administered by the local doctor for Harold to extract teeth, and the sickly smell of ether would drift down into the rest of the house, sending Ardotte scurrying outside for some fresh air. The recovery room, when such a luxury was needed, was Harold and Jean's bedroom, on the other side of the 'waiting room' which was actually the front hall. Other patients sat nervously in this waiting room, surrounded by old magazines—The Bulletin, National Geographic, Homes and Gardens, and the Mandrake and Ginger Meggs comics for the children—and, if they were early on the list of appointments, watching buckets of blood-stained towels being whisked out to the back of the house for Jean to soak, wash and prepare for the next victim.

This dental practice was very much a two person business.

WILDERNESS

In 1932, Ardotte, dressed in brown uniform and yellow straw hat, started school life at 'The Wilderness School' in Medindie, and her proper name, 'Margaret' always reduced to 'Margie' was used at last. A year before this her big sister, Helen, had left Woodlands and no longer had to take the long tram trips to get there, and had settled into 'The Wilderness'. There was little change in Helen's uniform, still brown, with touches of blue, a yellow straw hat and brown gloves. But the 'Woodlands' badge, which was the Church of England Cross with the motto, *'Crucem ad Lucem'* of 'Woodlands' was changed for the 'Wilderness' badge of the Lion Rampant enscrolled by the words, *'Semper Verus'*—'Always True'.

'The Wilderness School' was, and still is, a non-sectarian school, founded by Miss Margaret Brown in 1884 to educate her youngest sister, Mamie, and a few other local girls. Soon all four sisters—Maggie, Annie, Winnie and Mamie—were all involved in developing the School into a popular girls' school, taking in boarders from the country, and little boys up to the age of eight years.

All four women developed a democratic approach to education, with a keen sense of fairness, and always the encouragement of the individual ability of each student. Miss Mamie gained a Bachelor Degree of Arts at the Adelaide University, quite unusual for a woman in those far off days. Her keen interest in different methods of education led her to the work of Maria Montessori, and she introduced this method into the early classes of the school. The wooden jigsaw puzzles of the map of the World, the red and blue measuring sticks for maths, and the sandpaper tactile numbers and letters are some of the education 'tools' that she imported from Italy to give her young students a keener interest in 'learning as play'. The development of each student at his or her own pace was also taken from Doctor Montessori's earlier work with intellectually disabled children. This method and the equipment can still be seen in use at the many 'Montesssori' schools that have grown up throughout Australia.

For the middle school students, Miss Mamie followed the teachings of Charlotte Mason, relying on the narration of lessons to sharpen the attention and listening skills of students, and of course terrifying the shy ones who had to stand in front of the class and 'tell back' what had just been read.

The teaching programs of 'The Wilderness' may have sometimes seemed to be a little unorthodox to the outside community, but without any enforced allegiance to a Church body, it became a unique form of education in Adelaide, the 'City of Churches'.

Adelaide had a strong Church of England based 'establishment' and all the non-Catholic private schools of Adelaide were connected to, and overseen by one of the Protestant Churches. Without this allegiance to a managing body, the Browns were free to follow their own ideas of education, and especially to develop their ideas of encouraging the growth of unique, capable and responsible young women. There was no set mould for the girls to conform to. The measure of success was whether you were doing your best, whether you were ensuring that your fellow students were OK, and whether you had the confidence to speak honestly and openly in any situation. There was an unusual freedom to daily school life. Rules and time-tables were there, of course, but the punishment for breaking any rules, or of anti-social behaviour, was usually time spent on your own in the Brown's drawing room, given time to think about where you went wrong. They were daunting half hours as more often than not another teacher would come into the drawing room for some reason, and then of course want to know why you were sitting there on your own. This lesson seemed to penetrate the teen-age mind-set more effectively with such a velvet glove approach.

SECTION 2
GROWING PAINS

SCHOOL

And so my schooling began, and continued for twelve years at the one school, 'The Wilderness'. The School property was made up of a two storey house in which the four Misses Brown lived, and a mis-matched collection of buildings including a stable, a loft, and an old tram-car, all lined up along the 'Running Track' which was also the venue for many sports days, and many grazed knees from falls on the fine gravel surface. All of this was set in a large rambling garden on one acre of land in the suburb of Medindie, two miles north of the city centre of Adelaide.

My school days were not particularly eventful, but the first day remains firmly in my memory. Two small girls, one with brown plaits, one with yellow, thinner but longer plaits, stood under the window of the Montessori room and agreed to be friends. Mary Robertson kept that friendship with me for five years until she was moved to the then *very* prestigious school of 'Woodlands', and as 'The Wilderness' was not seen to be a very high standing school in the social scale of Adelaide, our paths seldom crossed.

About that time I found another 'best friend' who, sadly for me, had another 'best friend' of her own. So we became a sometimes uneasy threesome with whom I never felt very secure. One girl, Sue, was innovative and interesting and a bit chubby, and her father was a lawyer, which really pleased my mother. The other, Wendy, was really attractive, glittering black eyes and very shapely legs, nice clothes and no father at all! which was a rare occurrence in those pre-war years. Each of their worlds seemed so much more exciting than mine, and each of them had plenty to say at all times; not a whisper of shyness between them. And we did have many good times together, they being the leaders, and me the small follower.

Sometimes we met half-way to school and rode our bikes together, racing down the final hill to the back gate of the school. On our way home we would stop at a little small-goods shop and pore over the halfpenny and penny trays of sweets, spending ages deciding which sweets were the best bargain to buy with the penny that we had to share between us. Occasionally we would take so long making our selections that the old man who ran the shop would go out the back to feed the cat or make a cup of tea, leaving us alone in the shop. That was the waited for moment of the whole exercise and we would each grab an extra jelly or toffee out of the halfpenny tray, giggling hysterically as we left our inadequate penny for the poor old shop-keeper. Why were we such nasty little 'college girls', especially when our School Motto distinctly said 'Always True'? But the daring and excitement of this mean little achievement kept us convulsed all the way home.

A SISTER, TWO BROTHERS, AND A CREEP

My sister Helen, three years my senior, was good at all sports: 'A' Tennis Team, 'A' Basketball Team, swimming and diving. She also had lots of friends, did well in exams, arranged flowers really well, and could go on outings with our brothers. Even though my nightly prayers finished with the compulsory line, '…*and thank you God for giving me such a lovely sister as Helen*' (and of course the obligatory'… *and make Margie a good girl*'), I spent my childhood green with envy, and churlish with resentment, of all her cleverness and fun. Too often I watched her go out with our brothers, and sometimes their friends, on horses or bikes, in the car to go sailing or even to dances. I was left with my mother who was always occupied sewing, talking on the telephone or having visitors.

"Just go and play quietly somewhere, Ardotte. Go and play tops!"

Once, I took great delight in hiding Helen's push bike when she was going out for a picnic with some school friends. Gleefully I watched her hunt all over the extensive garden, thinking I had fixed her this time. But of course she found the scarcely concealed bike without too much delay, and the only result was a furious sister, an angry mother, and even more hours of solitary play in the bougainvillea cubby with my teddy-bear.

My brothers also created many mixed emotions for me. They were eight and ten years older than me and seemed enormous. Sometimes, if I crept in a bit late for lunch, having stayed in the mulberry tree a bit long, one of these giants would roar at me:

"Ardotte! Look at your dirty hands. Go and wash those filthy finger nails, and while you're there make up your mind whether you want butter OR jam on your scones. You know you can't have both." It needed all my tremulous courage to sidle back into the dining room, my fingers pink with sand soap and scrubbing.

But when one of these same scary giants would say to me, "Hey George," (their friendly name for me) "I'll donkey you to school this morning" my little scrawny chest would be bursting with joy and pride. I would hope that the whole school was outside to see my amazing, gallant brother. But of course, nobody noticed, and the shy little brown-eyed girl slipped into her place in the school room without causing the slightest ripple of interest.

In the year 1936 there was a dreadful outbreak of Poliomy-elitis in Adelaide. So fearful were the symptoms and effects of this paralysing infection that schools were closed and we were sent our lessons by correspondence. We were totally isolated in our homes, and children were kept away from shops, beaches and anywhere where there may be risks of infection. It was terribly boring, except that, for me, it meant that my sister was home all the time and I had someone to play with. As the fear lessened, but we were still not back at school, some of her friends would come to our house, and then I was allowed to join in with them and even go for short bike rides with them. They were great times for me.

Much to my amazement I even got a prize from school! 'Ivanhoe' a tediously boring book by Walter Scott, was my reward for learning 'The Rime of the Ancient Mariner' off by heart! Not bad for a 10 year old.

But one incident stands out starkly in my memory of those school-free days. On one of the rare bike rides that I was invited to join with the older girls, we rode out to the 'trotting track,' an oval-shaped dirt track in the wide, empty paddocks that were about half a mile from our house. This track was used by Mr Webster to test and train his horses, his pacers, for the big races, 'the Trots', that were held every Saturday night. On this particular day, when I had been allowed to join my sister and her friends, we were happily racing each other around the trotting track, and we saw a man slowly riding around on his own. When he saw us he rode towards us. I could see a large pinkish, short pole emerging upwards from his bicycle seat. A bit puzzling. He came closer and rode alongside one of the older girls, grabbing her hand from her handlebar and saying:

"Come on, touch it, touch it!"

I had never seen such a thing, and when I realised that the 'pole' was a soft fleshy thing attached to the man's body, I was totally amazed.

But the older girl quickly snatched her hand back from his grip and sped off on her bike, followed by all of the other girls with my sister urging me to ride faster. Once we reached the safety of the nearest suburban street the girls hopped off their bikes and gathered in a wide-eyed, giggling breathless huddle, whispering together about their weird experience. I still had very little understanding of what had happened; at the age of 10 my knowledge of the male anatomy was zero. But the older girls all swore a pact of secrecy, and made it very clear to me that I was *never* allowed to say *anything* to *anybody* about what we had all just seen.

So passed my first experience of a paedophile.

FIRST KISS

I got reasonable results in the lower classes at school, but when it came to concentrated study in the 'exam classes' I rather fell behind and took two attempts to pass each level of the Public Examinations that we all had to sit for in the final three years of school. I could run and hurdle a bit, but always came second or third, never gaining the treasured blue ribbon. My tennis was rather basic, and my basketball (now called netball) was reasonable as long as I was given the position of 'attack wing'. But none of my efforts were good enough to get me into a team.

Then ballet started to creep into my life and, to my amazement, I was considered to be a capable dancer. My Ballet Mistress, Miss Joanne Priest, was quite generous in her praise of my abilities and told me that I had 'good timing, good *porte des bras* (arm movement), excellent *sautés* (jumps) and good musical understanding.' This was rare praise which I relished, and so ballet became my passion.

Of course, ballet was a girls-only activity, and my 'best friend' and her 'best friend' decided between themselves that at the age of almost fifteen I hadn't had any 'fun' and that it was time that I was kissed... by a boy!!!

So... a charity dance was to be held at the local Saint Andrew's Church Hall. Susan and Wendy put their heads together and agreed that Wendy would lend her boyfriend, Brian McK, to initiate me in the 'joys and delights' of kissing, and the Church Dance was the perfect time to do it. And it seemed that this idea of introducing a raw young girl to the mysteries of *boys* was agreed to by all concerned.

I felt particularly glum about the arrangement. I hadn't had too many romantic dreams up to now, and those that I had had certainly didn't involve an arranged liaison with someone else's boyfriend, kindly *lent* for the occasion.

The following Saturday was the dance and the Big Awakening was to follow the seventh dance, the dance that followed supper. In those days each girl at a dance had a little program card with a small pencil tied to it. It was the girl's lot to wait hopefully for boys—any boy—to come and write his name in her program, and so booking her for any dance that suited him. The breathless shame when the shyer girls had to admit to a few blanks in their program usually made the night a complete misery, and the dances that held no scrawled name in their program were spent in red-faced embarrassment sitting on the side-lines watching the other girls dancing happily, or hiding in the 'powder room' with the other 'wallflowers'. The 'fast' girls, of course, had no trouble filling their programs.

So, Sue and Wendy arranged that Brian would ask me for the seventh dance, and this was to be *my moment*.

But, a young, stocky, square-faced boy called John who had met me at Scottish dancing classes, had already booked me for the fifth dance, and I felt shyly excited about that. He was good-looking, didn't say much at all, and danced a good Highland Fling. Towards the end of our dance together, John steered me towards the side door of the hall, took my hand and, completely wordlessly, led me along the gravel path, through the Church gardens to a thick clump of bushes, and there beside some crumbling tombstones he proceeded to kiss me… *six times*! lips firmly closed but still proper kisses, on my mouth!… and still wordlessly!

My legs turned to jelly! Whoa-wheeeee! Is this what it is all about? Silently and still with no spoken word between us, we went back into the dance hall where supper was just about finished. I felt happily breathless, and filled with a giddy sense of excitement. Did I really have to go through with the other charade?

But being a shy and timid young thing, and not wanting to lose favour and go against my 'best friends' plans, I said nothing to them about that amazing happening and bravely waited for the next lesson to be carried out after Dance Seven.

And so, after a 'college trot' sort of dance with Brian, he led me down to the Walkerville Oval, and there, behind a raggedy hedge that concealed the local rubbish tins, he proceeded to give me a series of wet, sloppy, intrusive kisses. Yuk!

"There, Margie, now you know what it is all about. One day I will teach you a lot more".

Prophetic words… but that is another story.

The next day Sue's mother, who was one of the supper ladies at the dance, reproached me saying,

"I saw you go outside with that Prince Alfred's boy last night… for quite a long time!! Do you want me to tell your Mother?"

DAD

My father was a very important influence in my life. He was an interesting man—very different from the other fathers that I met through my school friends. He was seldom angry, never remote, spent a lot of time about the house and garden, usually whistling or quietly singing wherever he went. He was not a restrictive parent. We were allowed a lot of freedom and independence. He believed in looking at the 'calculated risks' involved in any plans we might have, and then mostly encouraging us to 'give it a go'. Other girls at school were often wishing that they had been born as boys. I couldn't see much point in that. Life seemed challenging enough to me without adding that complication.

Dad loved his work as a dentist, although it was a fairly grizzly and brutal activity in those far off days. He did all his own mechanical work in a little lean-to, leaky workshop that he had built beside the ivy-covered outdoor lavatory. He loved inventing things and creating interesting little working machines, sometimes with a purpose, and sometimes just for fun. He made a mechanical turning frame for winding the silk off the yellow cocoons from our multitude of silkworms that lived in boxes all over the bedroom that I shared with my sister; he made a stud for his collar out of a sixpence and a bit of spare silver from his workshop; electric lights for the doll's house that he had made for me out of a packing case; a perpetual motion machine driven by the sun, and the most dramatic of all, an electric egg-beater and this was 1938! The beater was a clever idea but it didn't last very long. It was made from strong wire bent into a loop, the motor was from an old vacuum cleaner and the mixing bowl was my mother's tall cylindrical shaped Royal Doulton china jug. A few servings of scrambled egg and a milk-shake came out of this contraption before a wrong twist of the beaters going at full speed shattered the rather precious jug.

Another useful initiative of Dad's was a coke burner which he balanced on the parcel rack at the back of our family car, somehow transferring gas to the engine in place of petrol which was, of course, very scarce during the War. For this exercise he needed the collaboration of one of his patients who was a mechanic. I could never understand how burning coke in a hot cylinder attached to the parcel carrier at the back of the car could actually push it along, even if not particularly quickly.

The Second World War brought many shortages into our normal daily lives in Australia, but one particular one that affected Dad's work prompted him to get inventing again.

Up until 1942 the artificial teeth that were used to make dentures were made of 'transparent porcelain' and came from America. With America entering the War after the bombing of Pearl Harbour in 1941, the supply of artificial teeth dried up very quickly. So Dad's creative energies got busy. He bought sheets of acrylic resin which came in clear and pink material and normally were used for the windows of aeroplanes. He moulded the acrylic into the various shapes of artificial teeth. It was reported in the local newspaper that,

'…(the teeth) could bite but lacked natural colour. He spent time and money with various fabric dyes but eventually bought a few pennorth of yellow ochre from the local ironmonger. He then obtained a satisfactory and natural effect by making the teeth in two layers with the colour showing faintly through the clear surface plastic.'

Again Jean became a useful part of his dental practice by being the first recipient of these homemade teeth, and also by being the model who demonstrated the prototype to his '*…somewhat sceptical fellow dentists.*' Sceptical maybe but they were convinced, and it was agreed that the new teeth were '*…less brittle than the transparent porcelain and could also be fashioned …(in colour and shape) … to the individual wearer.*'

Not being much of a businessman, Dad didn't get around to taking out a patent on his newest and most successful invention, and a dental mechanic in Melbourne with similar aspirations was able to set up a large operation and was soon

'…turning out 15,000 teeth a week, and Australia, thanks to war shortages, became self-supporting in the way of dentures.'

Camping trips for the whole family were a source of delight to my father – and usually a source of various levels of terror for me. Driving along the Great Ocean Road in the early 1930's, when that magnificent scenic road was just a narrow track clinging to the cliffs high above the Southern Ocean, was a trip I remember with dread. Fortunately we were travelling west to east, from Adelaide to Melbourne, so, keeping to the left hand side of the track, our wheels were not so likely to slip over the precipice. But at one point we had to cross a river with just two planks forming the roadway. With a trailer on behind, this was quite a tenuous exercise, and it took both boys to guide Dad as he manoeuvred the old Essex over this hazard.

Being the youngest and smallest member of the family, I always sat in the front seat of the car, between my mother and father. Of course, my view from there was of the instruments in the dash board in front of me. But my brothers made sure that I knew what was going on outside, particularly when there was a bush-fire in the distance on the horizon. They would give me graphic descriptions of how quickly it was coming towards us, and how widely spread it was and whether we would be able to race it to safety. I also had to sit uncomfortably with my short little legs straight out in front of me. The 'self-starter' was a modern innovation that now replaced the handle that stuck out from the front of the car and had to be manually and energetically wound to get the engine going. This new addition was located on the floor of the car, directly under where I was sitting. My brothers made it very clear to me that if my bare toe so much as touched that metal button the car would start going backwards and would not stop until we got back to the house at 159 Main North Road. Really scary stuff!

My father loved to explore remote places. When we lived at Glenelg he had a small dental practice at Kingscote, which was then a tiny settlement on Kangaroo Island, a day's journey by sea down St Vincent's Gulf and across the choppy seas of the Great Australian Bight to the little port. My sister remembers meeting Dad on the Glenelg jetty as he disembarked from the little coastal steamer, SS Karatta after it had made the long journey home again. Helen remembers this short, slender man, jauntily whistling as he walked towards her and Jean, his bag of instruments in one hand and a string of fresh whiting in the other.

Dad undertook another quite large adventure in 1928.

With five other men, two from Balaklava and the others ex-Balaklava, and in an *almost new* Touring Hudson, he drove across extensive sandy deserts to Alice Springs, out to Hermannsberg, and then by donkey out to Palm Springs, a hidden oasis about nine miles further on into desert country, which was spectacular but still dry and stony. The donkeys had to carefully pick their way along the dry rocky bed of the Finke River. The written report of this journey refers to Dad as '*the optimistic member of the party*', which now, in later years, I realise was his typical attitude to most things in life.

Travelling almost every day for three weeks the heavily laden, open sided, soft-top car carried the six men, their luggage, water, fuel and food through endless sand dunes and rocky tracks. They camped out each night, occasionally sleeping in the sheds of some of the remote stations that they passed by. These sheltered places gave them relief from the icy cold nights in the desert where, by about 4 am the camp fire had gone out, and some hardy person needed to get out of his sleeping bag and pile more wood on the fire.

They had a number of friendly encounters with Aborigines, although they had been warned,

'*whites always go around in pairs up in the danger zone, one to keep watch for blacks and the other to do the jobs*'.

They saw quite a lot of wild life, occasionally being able to shoot a wild turkey, a euro or a kangaroo rat to supplement their basic diet of the ten dozen eggs that they had brought with them. They had found that they needed to send some of their food on ahead by train to Oodnadatta so that they could pack the running boards with extra cans of petrol and water. Of course they blew a few tyres but there were no major mishaps on the whole of the 2,300 miles of this amazing journey.

The 15 page report of this quite adventurous trip—remember, no mobiles, no radio, no water, no maps,—was printed in instalments in the Balaklava paper, the Wooroona Producer. The editor commented that,

'….the article should prove most interesting as it is the Government's intention to make Palm Springs a great tourist resort.'

Unfortunately, nearly ninety years later, this dream has still not come to fruition.

The report ended with the statement that,

'the trip… leaves many pleasant memories of acquaintance with the far north of Australia, a place of vast distances, drought and stout hearts.'

I got a lot of learning from my Dad—practical things that have stayed with me all my life. He taught me to swim, to ride a bike, row a boat, grow vegetables and drive a car. My first effort at driving on the open road was when I was twelve!! Certainly it was on a country road, but the first thing I had to do was to drive across a train line, and that seemed very daunting. His main lesson to me was,

'If you drive for the comfort of your passenger you will be a good driver and you will also be a safe driver.'

I have often wished that some people who have driven me in their cars had had the same lesson!

My father talked to me about physics, chemistry, algebra and geometry. We had little conversations in Latin—all to do with a sailor, his parrot and a table that they sat on—and near—and under! He showed me how to build a camp fire, *and* to keep it alight; to make billy tea and damper, and how to find the South Pole by the stars.

He talked about bits of his own philosophy of life—and death...

"I believe that your immortality is the mark you have made while you are living," he said, "the way you have touched other people, the little something that you may have been able to teach to another human being... If it has been good for that person then your life has been worthwhile and you will in some way be remembered."

My father's immortality certainly lives on through me, and the threads of it continue, probably unknown to them, through my children and so on through their children. And I do believe that my Dad's idea of immortality is more powerful and more valuable and more worth striving for than the dream that we used to be taught in Church that one's spent spirit floats off into some sunny place called Paradise, looking to receive its eternal heavenly rewards, and relaxing for evermore.

MUM

And my mother? Well...

My mother had many interests—and house-keeping was not one of them. She was a good basic cook, enjoyed a bit of gardening, with Mr Wishart, the gardener doing all the 'heavy bits'. She made our clothes, and plaited horrible raffia hats for my sister and me. These peculiar head-pieces were covered with flowers which she embroidered in coloured raffia. They felt very *home-made* and were a bit of an embarrassment to wear, especially when it rained and they came up to a pointy peak in the top of the crown.

Mum was active in the Parents and Friends Union of The Wilderness School, and developed a great respect for the Misses Brown, so she seemed to know more of what was going on at the school than we did. One of her burning passions was the Country Women's Association, and a couple of days each week saw her spending the whole day in their club rooms where activities to support the wives of farmers living in remote areas of the State of South Australia were planned and carried out. Hand crafts and a 'round robin' letter that she wrote for those isolated women were my mother's main skills, (as well as talking), and during the long years of the Second World War, knitting scarves, balaclava hoods and mittens for 'our servicemen', and making yards and yards of knotted string camouflage nets kept her very busy. These nets would be draped around our living room, and tacked to the wooden mantel piece. We were all encouraged to 'knit a few rows or knot a few strings' in any spare moments between homework, music practice and washing up.

But maybe her greatest attribute, and one for which she was gratefully remembered by many of my brothers' and my sister's friends, was her ability to listen to young people when they needed someone to help them sort out some emotional problem. During the war years, and a few years following the end of the war, endless young service men, or their girl-friends, would sit and talk to my mother for hours, seeking her support, sympathy, and well-considered advice, as they tried to cope with the traumas and conflicts of active war service and the difficulties of their affairs of the heart, and the equal difficulties of resettling back into civilian life.

They all adored her—and my jealous little lonely heart

resented every one of them. Again, I seemed to be the smallest and most forgotten one.

So—did I learn things from my mother too?

Of course I did—maybe not so many positive and practical things as I did from my father, but the lessons are always there to be learnt, useful or not.

My mother played the piano extremely well, and many Sunday nights saw a group of young people singing enthusiastically around the piano, my mother very happily and comfortably playing the accompaniments. And this was one thing that I was able to join in with.

She certainly encouraged my piano studies, and I wasn't too bad on the piano, having no ability to memorise anything, but I had a surprising gift for sight-reading. This led me to spend minimum time on practising between lessons, although I got away with that quite easily because I would just put the appropriate number of minutes of practice in my record sheet, and my mother who was busy with her sewing or on the phone to someone would willingly sign whatever was before her. And this avoidance of hers led me to the most embarrassing award of my whole life.

At the annual break-up one year I received the prize, a book of the life of Franz Schubert, for 'the most practice for the year'! The prize was given to the pupil who had recorded the most practice time in her record sheet. I could hardly bring myself to creep up to the front of the room to receive this ill-deserved award.

The rather boring little book still sits on my bookshelf, somehow a reminder that cheating, even if you get away with it, brings such feelings of guilt and embarrassment that it is probably better to just put up with being a bit of a failure and bear the consequences rather than live with the niggling memory of doing the wrong thing. The evidence of that action has been sitting on my bookshelf for over seventy years!

My mother also encouraged me in my ballet classes, but I think that that was mainly because of the *nice* girls from *nice* families, including the daughters of the Lord Mayor of Adelaide, who were also students of Miss Joanne Priest's Ballet School. Once my passion for ballet was firmly established though, she seemed to lose interest in it. I was always a little sad that during the 15 years of stage performances in different theatres of Adelaide, including the Theatre Royal, and dancing to the State Symphony Orchestra conducted by Sir Bernard Heinze, my family were seldom, if ever, in the audience.

I was not, as I have said before, a brilliant dancer, and certainly never a star, and nor did I want to be. That would have been much too much pressure and responsibility for me. But I loved every minute of our long hours of rehearsals and training classes, the make-up, the costumes, the flood-lights, the close working together with the other dancers, and even the blisters on poor tortured feet. Joanne Priest, our ballet mistress was totally dedicated to producing serious ballet works for her very amateur but enthusiastic students. Her choreography was toned to our level of ability; her patience and encouragement were inspiring. She also educated us well in classical music and its history, in theatre and opera, literature and poetry. We even performed ballet simply to the spoken word.

She taught us discipline over our bodies and over our minds. She was never damning in her criticism, always strict, but constructive and ready with praise.

Joanne Priest was undoubtedly one of the key women in my life. At no time did she make me feel inadequate in any way. I was not a brilliant dancer, nor an outgoing actor, and yet Joanne would praise me for my 'musicality,' for my attention to detail, and always had me in the lead position for stage entrances, partly because I was the smallest in the class, but also, she always emphasised, because I could be relied on to get the timing and the steps exactly right.

But in the Adelaide of the 1940's and 50's the things my mother taught me *were* important. It *did* matter how you held your knife and fork, how you dressed, especially how you spoke. It *was* important to know the correct way to answer an invitation, who your friends were, and what school you went to, and even where you shopped. The word 'common' was often heard, always derogatory. State schools were *not* acceptable and were held out as a threatening alternative if homework wasn't done properly or uniforms weren't in good repair. Even my father joined in on that one,

"Alright, if you can't be bothered doing that essay properly I will send you to the Nailsworth School!"

Gulp! I usually felt confident that my mother would *never* let him do such a dreadful thing.

But when I was about fourteen my mother became desperately ill. By the time an ambulance took her to hospital, she had had a raging temperature and a blinding headache for the whole day and had sunk into a state of unconsciousness. She stayed that way for four long days. At last she was diagnosed with meningitis, a most dangerous infection in that early period of the Second World War in 1940. But a new miracle drug had just come into use in Australia—sulphanilamide—and after intense treatment with that wonder drug at the Infectious Diseases Hospital where she stayed, totally isolated for several weeks, my mother was eventually allowed to come home.

Perhaps a little to her surprise, I had taken over some of the cooking, with my father doing quite a bit of it as well, and I had the feeling that my mother was really starting to notice my existence for the first time. I think my sister must have been busy with her final school exams as I don't remember her playing a very big part in the domestic chores at that time. So it was a good time for me, as I was starting to feel that I *did have* some part to play in our family life.

COUSIN MARIE

Actually, my home life had taken a big jump for the better about a year prior to this.

My mother's brother, Keith, was tragically drowned when he fell out of a small boat crossing the wide, deep River Murray at Wentworth where he lived with his wife, Fonnie, and their two young sons and a very small daughter. Keith and some mates were coming home from a celebration at the local hotel, and when he stood up to wave to the family from the middle of the River, he toppled into the water and sank straight to the bottom. He had never learnt to swim. My Uncle Keith had always been a bit of a rolling stone, charming and loveable, but not too successful in life, and so his young family was left with very little money. There were no social services in those days, and my Aunt Fonnie was left with the responsibility of going back to work as a nurse, and also to manage three small children on her own. My parents decided to offer to have the youngest child, Marie Jean, to stay with us in Adelaide. They made arrangements for her to go to school with me, and were happy to support her until she was old enough to manage on her own. It was a big offer, and Aunt Fonnie accepted it. Her small daughter had no say in it whatsoever.

Later, Marie told me that her mother had asked her,

"How would you like to go to Adelaide, Marie?"

Marie thought that could be a nice outing. No one mentioned to her that, as she boarded the enormous bus that was to take her to her new life in Adelaide, it wasn't just for the day. It was for good—or at least for the next ten years! (This seemed to be happening in many parts of Australia to many unsuspecting kids!).

For me, the arrival of this very small, *very* pretty young cousin from the bush meant the arrival of a younger sister that I had always needed. Marie was just seven years old. Shy, but quietly self-contained, amazingly accepting of the rather startling new life that she had been thrown into, willing to help in all ways, she stoically went off to a comparatively grand private school, with new uniform, hat, and gloves. I am not sure if any of us stopped and thought about what a dramatic change this was for one small girl who had been taken so suddenly from her family, and the bewilderment and losses that she had to cope with at that time.

Although there were six years between us, Marie and I became very close friends. I probably neglected her shamefully at school, but at home we spent many happy times together. We shared a bedroom, although Marie, coming from the bush, was not impressed with my cat often sharing bed space with me. We often rode to school together, and due to an arrangement my father had with one of his patients who couldn't afford to pay for her dental treatment, we took singing lessons together. I had someone to be a 'Big Sister' to, and as a consequence, I guess, had someone to fetch and carry for me a bit.

One very useful bargain I struck up with Marie involved getting my lunch cut every day. In our bathroom there was a rusted gas burner that heated the water for showers or baths. Dad had covered the hole in this ferocious burner with a flattened tooth-paste tube so that, mostly, it could be lit without blowing back and making a terrifying noise, before, we presumed, exploding and taking the whole house with it. Marie couldn't bear the trauma of this exercise and would even have a cold shower rather than risk being blown sky high. As I was a bit taller than her, and a bit older though no braver, I was able to adjust the toothpaste tube so that I could light the gas without too many blowbacks. To bribe me to do this for her, Marie would cut my school lunch each day, a great arrangement from my point of view.

And then one day, when I opened my lunch box to extract my sausage sandwich, I found it wrapped in a piece of paper with a poem written on it:

> 'Margie had a little cat,
> Her cousin shot it dead.
> And now she takes poor puss to school
> Between two lumps of bread'

Marie had exacted her revenge!

WAR

In 1945 the Second World War finally came to a close, but only in Europe – leaving a waste land of once beautiful cities, and the lush countryside of the Continent and of England, bombed and desecrated almost beyond recognition, and leaving the lives of the people of many countries shattered and damaged almost beyond repair. Three long months later, after many more casualties, more loss of life, and the horrendous devastation of the two atomic bombs dropped by the Americans on the Japanese cities of Hiroshima and Nagasaki, the Japanese emperor finally, on 15 August 1945, surrendered on behalf of his humiliated country.

The war-shocked men and women of the three armed services, and those from the prisoner of war camps, gradually came straggling back to Australia to begin the next traumatic period of their lives, trying to settle back into a dramatically changed civilian world again. Women who had learned to manage their lives without the support of their menfolk; children who had lived without a father for four or five years; elderly parents who now had trouble recognising the gaunt and moody son they had last seen as an eager, excited young soldier going off to save the world, all had to learn to cope with the pressure of their traumatised men, changed forever by the shocking experiences they had fought to survive.

Australia was on the other side of the world when the war first broke out, but in our seemingly insignificant and secure part of the world we were certainly not untouched by the privations and changes that happened very quickly. The day that Great Britain declared war on Germany, Friday 3rd September 1939, was a dramatic and sobering day for all of us. Even as a child of thirteen I was suddenly aware of the solemnity that had fallen all around me as the voice of Mr Menzies, our Prime Minister, resounded through the house announcing in very dark tones:

'Fellow Australians, it is my melancholy duty to inform you officially that, in consequence of the persistence of Germany in her invasion of Poland, Great Britain has declared war upon her, and that, as a result, Australia is also at war. No harder task can fall to the lot of a democratic leader than to make such an announcement. Great Britain and France, with the co-operation of the British Dominions, have struggled to avoid this tragedy. They have, as I firmly believe, been patient; they have kept the door of negotiation open; they have given no cause for aggression. But in the result their efforts have failed and we are, therefore, as a great family of nations, involved in a struggle which we must at all costs win, and which we believe in our hearts we will win.'

That same night, at our house, my grandmother, Sophie Mackie Tuck, aged 72, quietly died in her sleep.

As I didn't understand too much about war and all its horrific ramifications at that stage of my young life, the loss of my grandmother was the saddest thing that had ever happened to me. My Granny Tuck was the one person in my small world who seemed to notice that I existed. She sat in her rocking chair on our back veranda, me perched on her knee, listening, enthralled, as she sang endless songs to me, always followed by a story. She brushed my very long, thick, tangly hair, again making a wonderful story of the horse and plough having to get through a field of knobbly stumps... and every time that she hit a tangle in my hair and gently pulled it undone... she would describe the shape and the ruggedness of each new 'stump' that the horse and plough were pulling out

Granny taught me to knit, and we would have knitting races together, and somehow I used to win on each row! But she could also be a little scary. She was a rigid member of the Church of Christ and when she came to our house for Sunday dinner after attending her Church for Morning Service, we were not allowed to sew, play cards and no playing the piano, not even scales, (only hymns of course), and *certainly* no outside games or frivolity on her Sabbath. And the one time that I was in really big trouble with her was when I brushed the breadcrumbs off the dining-room tablecloth, using the little brass crumb tray and brush that were the normal instruments for clearing the table, and I then threw the crumbs into the fire.

Granny was horrified.

"No, no, no," she called sharply, "that bread is the body of Christ. To burn it is a sin against Christ. Don't ever do that again!"

And of course, I never have. Even a piece of burnt toast brings back to me that uncomfortable moment of offending my beloved

Granny, even though it was followed by a warm, forgiving hug.

And so, when my Granny died the night that war was declared, I was doubly devastated at losing my one true friend and supporter, and my small world seemed to fall inwards around me.

My teenage years from 13 to 19 were spent in the shadow of our world at war. In Australia the coming of war quickly started to change our lives. Fear for England, which we always referred to as 'our Mother Country', was uppermost in people's minds. Australia was isolated and seemingly safe, but the Mother Country must be defended at all costs. Young men lined up to enlist in the three Armed Services. Sad farewells from mothers, stoic handshakes from fathers, and tearful embraces from sweethearts were regularly seen at the Adelaide train station. Frightening stories in the newspaper and the news-reels told of bombs falling in England, of Germany advancing rapidly through Europe; Poland, Holland, Belgium and then beautiful, exotic France were all swept through and over by Hitler's massive, heavy-booted army. Our teachers at school would read out tragic stories of personal courage and loss that came from the countries that were struggling for their lives.

The War Effort in Australia began in earnest. Black-out curtains were put up on every window, car lights were dimmed with brown paper. Ration coupons were issued to each family for almost everything, butter, sugar, tea, meat, eggs. All these things were needed for the survival of our troops. Petrol was heavily rationed, shops carried scant stock and even dress material was rationed as all cotton and wool were needed for uniforms for the fighting men. We recycled every possible thing; silver paper rolled into balls, soft-drinks cans, bottle tops and metal containers were melted down to be used in ammunitions. Fruit cakes were baked and sewn up in calico to send to isolated troops. Socks, scarves and balaclavas were knitted in khaki and navy blue for the men serving in the cold winters of England and at sea in unknown places. Everyone was involved in 'The War Effort' and each of us was silently grateful that we were so far away from the terrifying areas of war.

And then on February 19th 1942, unbelievably and without any warning, the Japanese Air Force dropped bombs on Darwin, Australia's most northern town. Shock and fear were everywhere.

"How could Australia be so blatantly attacked? What would become of us all?"

Food shortages became more intense. Growing home produce became a priority. The 'Austerity Campaign' urged us to save and re-use everything possible. Gas and electricity were rationed, and Daylight Saving was introduced for the very first time in Australia. The plan was that we would have our evening meal while the sun was still shining and then we could be in bed before it was necessary to turn on lights. Rationed gas became a bit of a problem in the Frayne household as the gas was turned off at 6.30 each evening, and Dad often didn't get home from his City practice till 7 o'clock. Fortunately we lived at the top of a small hill and the remnants of gas left in the pipes floated their way through, forming a very small flame, in our old gas stove top, but not enough to burn in the oven.

So to heat up Dad's belated dinner it was often necessary to light up the old wood stove that had lain idle in our kitchen for many years, covering the plateful of food with a saucepan lid and putting it in the lukewarm oven for half an hour and producing the slightly shrivelled meat and three veg that was the usual meal that we had every night.

In fear of invasion from the Japanese, names on railway stations were blacked out so that air-borne invaders landing on our shores would not know where they were and would not know which direction to take to carry out their attacks, and permits were needed for anyone wishing to cross the borders between the States. Air raid shelters were built under many homes and slit trenches were dug at schools and in public places, and we all received smallpox injections to help us with-stand the inevitable infection that we were bound to receive from the 'Yellow Peril'.

The Black Market flourished. American soldiers, with their abundance of supplies, cigarettes, clothing coupons and particularly nylon stockings, were hot favourites amongst the young women, but they were also increasingly unpopular with the young, not so well equipped Australian Service personnel who felt overshadowed by these well turned out 'foreign' soldiers.

All this seemed fairly exciting to this naïve sixteen year old. If I saw a couple of American soldiers chatting on the street corner I would pause and pretend to be interested in a nearby shop window just so that I could listen to their American accent. But my excitement waned dramatically when, one day as I was helping my father in his surgery, I overheard a conversation between him and one of his patients:

"So, Mr Frayne, do you think the Japanese will get down here, as far as Adelaide?"

I waited for my father's usual jocular response – but:

"Yes, Mrs Harris, - I'm afraid they will now."

This from my father – the cheerful optimist! Again a haunting fear settled around me, and silently I followed even more closely all news bulletins and daily reports of the War, the casualties, the losses and the atrocities being committed in the South Pacific against the local indigenous people, especially the women of Papua New Guinea and the Solomon Islands. But still I found no-one with whom I could share the burden of these fears, so I silently fretted over them and waited for the worst to happen.

There were no heroic medals bestowed on or earned by members of my family. My older brother, Bruce, completed his

Dental Degree early in the War, and immediately enlisted in the RAAF. His profession gave him the rank of Flight-Lieutenant and he looked wonderful in his smart navy blue uniform. He was sent to England to operate a mobile dental unit, a great, long, well-equipped trailer which he drove to all the RAF units in England, spending time in London when the Germans were sending the 'buzz-bombs' over the Channel to wreak havoc on the citizens of England. The buzz-bombs were unmanned planes loaded with explosives and they were timed to cut out anywhere over London. As the civilians heard the engines buzzing overhead they would wait and listen breathlessly to try to work out where this lethal mini-plane would eventually crash, knowing that there would be death and wreckage wherever it landed. My brother said that if you heard the engine cut out immediately above you, you knew that you were safe this time as the little machine would then glide for a short distance before it crashed to do its damage.

My younger brother, Keith, served briefly and, I think, half-heartedly, in the Militia, and was fairly quickly discharged after a serious bout of meningitis.

In 1944, during the last stages of the War, I attended Science lectures at the Adelaide University. My mother was very keen on education for women and, for no good reason, she was convinced that I would become a scientist. I seemed to have different ideas… I failed every subject!! Ballet was still my all consuming passion, and I spent many disciplined but happy hours at rehearsals, the great reward being a four or five day season of performances, presenting the original ballets that were carefully and thought-fully choreographed by Miss Priest, and with all the glamour of beautiful costumes, glamorous stage make-up and spotlights. Most of these performances raised funds for the ever-needful War Effort. They were always performed to live music, including the South Australian Symphony Orchestra, conducted by Sir

Bernard Heinze, a noted Melbourne conductor. Each performance was a really exciting experience and far outweighed any interest in studies at university, including the male dominated community that existed at all the lectures.

So then, having shown no academic skills whatsoever, and entirely due to my mother's influence through her Country Women's connections, I was given a job in the laboratory of Michell's wool mongering and tanning factory where I earned one Pound ten Shillings a week. And there I stayed, still living at home, reasonably well occupied, not learning a great amount, ballet still my first love, for the next four years, until the coming of marriage gave me an excuse to leave work and, at the age of twenty-four to leave home.

THE PATHWAY TO MARRIAGE

After my half-hearted response to my introduction to the 'delights' of being kissed by a boy, and as there seemed to be no further interest from the chunky, but silent Prince Alfred boy, John, who had just pipped Brian at the post of being my First Experience, I took very little interest in any boys at all. A few came by for a bit, but nothing of great interest. Dates were arranged for me, including a much sought after one to the 'Blue and White', the most prestigious dance of the year, held in the grand old main hall of St Peter's College. But as this particular date for me had been arranged by our ambitious mothers neither Des, the young man in question, or I were the slightest bit interested in each other. But those were the days when you actually did what your parents arranged for you, at least as far as they could tell. In this instance, Des was much more interested in his long term love, a girl from my school who I liked very much, though Des's mother definitely did not. So with everyone in agreement, Des spent most of the dances with Rose, until he was whipped off at midnight by his determined and very controlling mother, leaving me and Rose to spend the next couple of dances in the 'powder room' waiting for our own parents to pick us up at the normal 1.00 am finishing time.

So ballet and a bit of school work, a bit of sport and Friday night Ballroom Dancing classes kept me happily entertained without the complication of a serious boy thing.

But then along came Peter.

These were the War years, and young men could join the Navy at the age of 17. Peter had finished his schooling at St Peter's College and had gone straight into the Australian Navy. We met at a friend's birthday party. He looked great in his tight, navy blue sailor's top, white collar and navy blue trousers with the seven folds that represented the Seven Seas. He seemed to think I was a bit interesting and started to invite me to the cinema and trips to the beach He was thoughtful and considerate, earnestly serious, and led me gently through the various stages of boy/girl stuff. I thought he was okay, if a bit moody, but my mother didn't much like him... his father had an orange orchard, so he was only a 'blockie', and of German descent at that!

Then at 18, Peter went off to the war. He spent his first year sitting on a small ship, HMAS 'Kookaburra', protecting the boom cable across the entrance to the Darwin Harbour, and waiting for the next wave of Japanese planes to follow up their disastrous bombing of that isolated and vulnerable town. The first bombing of Darwin, totally unexpected and totally devastating was on February 19th 1942, and was followed by many more raids which caused wide spread death and damage and extended as far south as Katherine, 300 kilometres south of Darwin.

But this was now 1944 and as the Japanese forces were concentrating their efforts in Papua New Guinea the skies over Darwin were very quiet. So occasionally the young sailors would be free to play water polo in the warm milky waters of the Darwin Harbour, always with a couple of the crew, rifles poised, watching out for passing crocodiles. As the Japanese air-raids appeared to have stopped over the north of Australia, Peter then changed ships and was sent up to the Pacific Islands on HMAS Shropshire.

But for Peter this was another face of war altogether. By this time the Japanese were getting desperate to hold their ground in the Islands to the north of Australia and they trained young Japanese airmen to dive-bomb and crash into the Australian and American fleets. Those fleets were supporting the foot soldiers who were slogging through mud and jungle, rain and fever, snakes and scorpions, trying to eradicate the Japanese Army that was threatening to overtake Australia.

These 'suicide bombers' would fly over a ship with the sun directly behind the plane, making it a dazzling and near impossible target for the gunners to aim at. The bomber would then suddenly dive, nose first, and crash into any part of the deck of the ship, causing huge loss of life and often loss of ship.

After the War these terrifying episodes affected Peter badly.

"They're coming out of the sun, they're coming out of the sun," he would scream, coming out of a restless sleep, and then heart-breaking sobs would shake his body for hours after.

Alcohol became Peter's escape from these nightmare memories, and gradually his moods and his drinking became too much for this inexperienced nineteen year old young woman, and we gradually drifted apart.

Now Peter had a best friend called Jim Muirhead......

It was Easter 1946. On Good Friday my family was packing up to go to our shack at Aldgate in the Adelaide Hills. A tall, not too bad-looking, fair-haired young man arrived at our house on his bike, carrying a brown paper bag of fruit.

"Hullo, Mrs Fwayne, my Mum has sent you some apwicots fwom her twee," said this chap, who seemed to know my sister, and vaguely knew me through his friend Peter.

"Oh, Jimmy, how kind of her," said my mother, "but what are you doing here? I thought you were rowing in the King's Cup on the Nepean River in Sydney." (*How on earth would she know that?*)

"Oh, Mrs Fwayne, poor me. I was meant to be wowing in the University Eights, but I got a hernia when I was lifting the boat out of the wiver and one of the other cwew members dwopped his end of it, and I took the full weight of it and that caused this silly hernia. So I'm not allowed to wow till I've had it fixed and I'm not allowed to do *anything*. It's so borwing, and I am weally miswable."

"Why, Jimmy, that's too bad," and after a moment, "how about coming to Aldgate with us for Easter. It's only the girls and Mr Frayne and me going. You know, it's a bit like camping, wood stove, kerosene lanterns, beds in an old train carriage, and a nice wood fire. Plenty of blackberries to pick, though. What do you think? You would be very welcome."

As I listened to this interchange I thought, *What was my mother thinking of?* I supposed this odd chap would be someone for my sister, Helen, to mess around with. Certainly not my idea of fun, with that silly lisp.

Well, Jim seemed to think it was a good idea, because he raced home on his bike, packed his gear and was back in half an hour.

The weather was great, and we did seem to have fun. My sister seemed to have other interests that Easter, so we didn't see much of her, but another young man, Tom, called in to the shack on his push bike, and Tom, Jim and I formed a cheerful threesome, picking blackberries, playing a bit of tennis and going for long walks. On one occasion we came to a long steep hill, and as I got slower and slower, Jim picked me up in his arms and carried me the last half of the climb. Poor hernia!!

The next day Tom left on his bike to go home. As is usual at Easter, a big, shiny, perfect full moon came up over the hills. Jim suggested that we go out to the gate to have a better look at the moon. It was brilliant, and I gazed enrapt, enjoying the friendliness of this shared moment. Jim turned me gently towards him, and holding me in the warmest, kindest embrace, kissed me firmly and took a deep breath, and said,

"I think I may be falling in love with you."

Well, that just flustered me completely, and with a most unromantic attitude I said,

"Oh, go on… It's just the full moon making you a bit crazy."

Amazingly Jim didn't seem to be at all offended, gave me another, smaller kiss and off we went to our beds at either end of the old train carriage that formed the main part of that wonderful, old, primitive shack tucked in amongst the eucalypts and gorse bushes of the Adelaide Hills.

Over the next few months Jim visited me occasionally, took me out on his Army BSA motorbike, chatted happily to my mother, made me laugh on many occasions and altogether was quite fun to be with. But his awkward, hesitant, occasional question of "did I love him a *little* bit?" brought from me the damning reply … "yes, a little bit—sort of like a brother!"

Jim was into his second year of Law. He had done one year of his law Degree at the Adelaide University before spending the next three years of his life in the Army, first in the jungles of Queensland and then in the mud and slush and horror of Papua

New Guinea and the Solomon Islands. He didn't have much time to waste on an indecisive young woman, even if she was small, brown and cuddly. His interest in me may have been beginning to wane a little.

About this time, my father took me on a short holiday to Broken Hill, and I had time to think a bit. Quite suddenly I found that I was thinking a lot about Jim… and 'brothers' didn't seem to come into my feelings at all this time—and I couldn't wait to get back to Adelaide to tell him.

So, a couple of days later we were back at the Aldgate shack again with my family, and Jim and I went for a long rambling walk through the creeks and blackberries. It started to rain, quite heavily, and Jim found a little shelter for us deep in under some bushes. Shivering together there, I was brave enough to whisper, "I really did miss you while I was in Broken Hill, and… I think I really *do* love you… and not just like a brother at all!"

He seemed quite pleased.

We eventually announced our engagement on the 11th December 1948, but it was a long road before we could finally get married. Jim's greatest concern was to finish his Law Course, *and* pass his final exams which were not until November 1949. His father's greatest concern was that we should not consider marriage until Jim could afford to buy a house for us *freehold*!!!

Jim's mother was probably just plain concerned about everything to do with her only son leaving home so soon after miraculously returning relatively unscathed from the jaws of battle in the Pacific. I just wanted to be safely and securely married to this gorgeous, exciting man as soon as it could possibly be done.

My mother was delighted with our engagement. She adored Jim, he would soon be a lawyer, and he was from the Butler/Muirhead clan, a large and well-respected family group in the

Medindie/Walkerville area of Adelaide, and best of all, he made her laugh.

It was an action-packed fourteen months ahead of us.

Jim spent the next 14 months continuing his full-time work as an article clerk, attending lectures at the Adelaide University, and studying at all hours of the night. He didn't have much time or thought for the trappings that went with weddings.

But my mother found plenty for us both to do. The first thing that she got busy with was creating the best *trousseau* possible for this mousey little daughter of hers who was at last showing a bit of promise by marrying a most eligible young bachelor.

The *trousseau*, or 'glory box', was a very important part of the responsibilities of a bride-to-be. It consisted of all the 'manchester' items needed in setting up a new home, and also enough lingerie, both underwear and nightwear, that a young bride would require for her first few years as a responsible wife.

So with an open cheque book, a little reluctantly handed over by my father, Mum gathered together beautiful Irish linen sheets and pillowcases, each embroidered in pale blue thread, cut-embroidered linen tablecloths of various sizes with matching linen napkins, bath towels, tea-towels, and monogrammed guest towels. She ordered three sets of exquisitely lace-appliqued night-dress and matching gown, 'scanties', petticoat and camisole, all made in silk satin. To be useful, I made a couple of the lingerie sets myself, one of them from a white silk parachute that my previous boyfriend, Peter, had souvenired after the War and had given to me some time earlier. No doubt he had had some fancy ideas himself of seeing some unknown parts of me through this amazingly strong but surprisingly diaphanous fabric.

My mother also called in the help of a couple of her friends at the CWA to embroider some of the linen napkins, and monogram them with a very elegant 'M', while she also made a set of table mats with matching serviettes, and crocheted neat edges around each of them. All of these items were made of a suitably acceptable ecru linen. It was of great importance to have a good collection of high quality articles to display to 'the Aunts'. These were all of the Butler 'girls', Jim's mother and her six sisters, plus a few nieces.

Jim completed his final exams, but had several weeks to wait for the results, so he was not too relaxed over the Christmas period, but as our wedding was to be in February we then started the rounds of pre-wedding parties. There was a Bottle party for us both, the guests each bringing something alcoholic in a bottle for our empty cellar and, amongst much hilarity, his mother gave us a bottle of tomato sauce. Then for the bride there was a Kitchen tea, a Bathroom shower, a Pantry party, all attended by girl-friends, cousins and aunts who brought appropriate little gifts to each party. And at each one of these gatherings there was a display and showing of *The Trousseau*. My mother was so proud, and she was especially happy on the day 'the Aunts' came. They just *had* to be impressed at the enormous amount of household supplies that I was bringing to make 'their' Jimmy happy and comfortable, and, of course, to save him a lot of money.

And so the time fled by. My sister helped me to buy the material for the wedding gown. It was rather nice taffeta and satin cream silk, but Jim's mother, Mrs Muirhead as she was to me at that time, thought I should have had one of the Aunts to help me with such a major exercise. Helen and I thought we did quite a good job on our own, and between us and the dressmaker we designed a quite elegant wedding dress that snuggled neatly into my 24 inch waist and rustled romantically as I paraded up and down the passage. It was a happy co-operative time for us both.

And so, after all these giddy preparations, the time came for me to leave my childhood home and to take on the wonderful role of the *wife* of my beloved James Muirhead LLB.

SECTION 3
MARRIAGE, MOTHERING AND MOPING

SAFELY MARRIED

On Saturday February 4th 1950 my married life began.

Jim had been discharged from the Army in the early months of 1946, and over the next three years had managed to complete his Law degree. He had been accepted into the Law firm where he had done his Articles for four years, earning a Two Pound 'bonus' each Christmas, his father having paid three hundred Pounds for the privilege of having his son articled to this firm of Thomson, Buttrose, Ross & Lewis. Jim had a BSA Army motorbike for transport and almost no money in the bank. My mother owned a maisonette which we were able to rent, considering ourselves supremely lucky as, in the extremes of housing shortages following the War, most of our married friends had to occupy the spare room in their parents' homes, or, at best, a room or two in someone else's house.

Our Wedding Day was bright and sunny. Preparations buzzed all around me. In amongst having my hair done, a first ever facial and my nails shaped and polished I was instructed by my mother to:-

"Go to the Church, dear, and thank all Jim's Aunts who seem to be organising all the flowers. I'm sure its very kind of them."

My cousin, Marie was my bridesmaid and I sat between her and my father as we were driven to St Andrew's Church in Walkerville. My cousin asked me if I was feeling nervous at all, and I sombrely said "Certainly not!" whereupon Marie looked at the gypsophila vibrating violently in my wedding bouquet and raised her eyebrows, saying, "So I see!"

I managed to walk safely down the aisle, firmly supported by my father's strong arm, and after that I remember very little. My only interest was this tall, smiling man standing beside me, placing the simple gold ring on my finger, saying whatever the priest was telling us to say. This man who was going to be my companion for the rest of my life.

Choir boys sang, and the Church bells pealed gaily. People smiled and waved and confetti went down the neck of my taffeta and satin bridal gown.

Then finally, "One more photo please," and we were in the car, together, just the two of us, at last. I leaned over to give my brand new husband a hug and a kiss…

"At last we are married"… but, with a little nudging shrug, he responded ,

"Look, I just need to spend a bit of time thinking about the speech I have to make"!

Oh! … Oh dear! I wasn't quite sure that this was how married life should start. My apparently naïve belief that I was the centre of his universe, that after a very long two years of waiting, the two of us now becoming husband and wife, at last, was the most important thing that could happen to us on this Special Day, was clearly not quite the top-shelf priority that I thought it was. And this private moment of joy and fulfilment seemed to be set aside to give thinking time to *his* wedding speech!

Yes, I had a lot of growing up to do – and it all starts *now*, Mrs Muirhead.

But our wedding party *was* fun. 'Cousins, dozens of cousins', lots of aunts and uncles and a few friends made me feel ten feet tall, and so proud to now belong to this wonderful man. There were kisses and hugs aplenty, something else I wasn't good at, but would gradually grow used to, marrying into the Butler/Muirhead clan where kisses were frequent and mandatory. And Jim *did* make a wonderful speech and had everyone laughing heartily and all were full of admiration for him, with me his greatest admirer of all.

We had a two week honeymoon, firstly driving up to Mount Barker in the Adelaide Hills in one of Dad's cars, using the rationed petrol coupons that my father had saved for us. We spent a couple of days in an old country pub. I was very shy and embarrassed to be seen with a man, and going *together* into a bedroom! And then next morning at breakfast, seated at a table just for two, everyone seemed to stare at me, almost with question marks over their heads.

'*Little do you know,*' I thought in silence and some secret relief, '*I got my dates all wrong!*'

We walked for miles around those beautiful hills, and, the 'highlight' of that weekend? We visited a sausage factory, witnessing the whole process of sausage-making from squealing pig to flabby colourless sausage! Um… not the most romantic part of our honeymoon.

Ten days at an old traditional pub in Robe, a small holiday town on the rugged coast of the South East of South Australia was much more relaxing and normal. One startling moment came when a housemaid unexpectedly barged into our room, and we were still in bed – just the two of us! In the same bed! I blushed to my toenails.

But that was a very happy time—lovely days on the beach, long walks – a few games of tennis which stupidly I won! (another quick lesson on what *not* to do), and lots of talking and loving.

After the long hot bus trip back to Adelaide we moved straight into our little maisonette at Number 4 Gordon Street, Grassmere, and real married life began.

And it was *wonderful*. At last we were really on our own, away from the daily influence of parents. And although at times I felt that I was simply playing 'grown-ups' in my domestic life, it was just the two of us, planning, laughing, doing our separate jobs and enjoying the discovery of our close need for each other, and the gifts we each brought into this new and wondrous relationship.

I dreamt of our lives going on like this for ever.

And for six months it did. Jim's work was demanding and at times overwhelming for a young lawyer, five and a half days a week in the 'Firm' in Waymouth Street in Adelaide where he had done his four year term of Articles. Travelling on his Army BSA motorbike he appeared in the Magistrate's Courts of Port Adelaide and Gawler. He amused my mother, and me of course, with the stories of his not always successful appearances in UJS's (Unsatisfied Judgements), including:

"...And Mrs Fwayne, even though I told the Magistwate that my client fell off his bike and was lying on the woad like a *squashed apwicot...* he still got fined for careless widing."

My mother adored him.

Jim's weekly pay was Five Pounds Ten Shillings and the basic wage at that time, 1950, was Five Pounds Seventeen and Sixpence! So my role in the marriage felt wonderfully important, budgeting to house-keep on less than the basic wage.

Thirty five shillings went on the rent of our little half home which was owned by my mother. I carefully noted every penny that I spent on food and other little bits, and painted small cylindrical tins so that, weekly, I could put in each tin a two-shilling piece for the milk, the paper, the bread and the electricity. Proudly I recorded a saving of ten shillings at the end of some weeks.

I took a rather scary job doing a random survey of houses in the nearby suburbs. It involved knocking on stranger's doors and asking the householder to record, for a week, every time the family listened to the radio and also which station they were listening to. Of course, the reception I received was rather varied, but some people were kind and took a survey book. For this I received two shillings for every completed book that was returned to the central office. So I didn't actually make much difference to our budget. But I did have to grapple with my natural shyness each time I knocked on a new door, and I found that I *could* talk to complete strangers when I really had to. But I didn't like it much.

MOTHERING

And then, in August 1950, these halcyon days seemed to be put on hold.

I had reason to visit the family doctor, to be told, after a very embarrassing examination, that I was definitely pregnant! Of course, this should be the most joyous news that a young bride can receive. Why was I so devastated by it?

Poor Jim came home from work to find me in tears on the bed. When I sniffled at him that I was pregnant his face lit up with amazed joy. He had always feared that he would not be able to have children, or at best only have one, like his own state of lonely childhood that he had not enjoyed too much. When he tried to soothe and comfort me I could only gulp that I was feeling sick, I didn't want a fat tummy, and if it could turn out to be a kitten I wouldn't mind so much!!!

That must have been a pretty miserable attitude for a young husband to live with. I didn't really deserve the patient, thoughtful care that Jim gave me over the next seven and a half months. His father, Bonnie Muirhead, a delighted grandfather-to-be, gave us money to help us buy a car, a fairly ancient Vauxhall, as 'young pregnant women should *not* ride on the back of motorbikes'. Someone in the family lent us a cot, another a crib, another a changing table. Our lean-to sleep-out was turned into a nursery, Jim painting and cleaning on his day and a half weekends. I, of course, couldn't bear the smell of paint, so no help there. But I did make the curtains and numerous minute Viyella nightdresses and sometimes tried to respond to everyone else's enthusiasm for this little disaster that was about to upturn my life.

The baby was due on April 1st—April Fools' Day – no significance, of course. But time went on and not a sign of a contraction or any other symptoms that I had read of in Dr Grantley Dick-Read's book about child birth.

Then on Wednesday April 11th a few niggly pains started to emerge. By 7.30 that night we decided 'it was time'. And into the Vauxhall I heaved myself, with a huge suitcase filled with all the things the hospital had listed: binders and safety pins, pads, nursing bras, Agarol and Solyptol for me. Nappies and nighties, singlets both cotton and woollen, bonnets and booties for the baby-to-be, and soothing creams for the enormous lump in my over bulging stomach.

Sixty or so years ago child birth was treated very differently from now. Husbands were whisked out of sight as soon as possible. Enemas, shaving and more embarrassing pokes and examinations were imposed on the new mother-to-be. Very little communication came from anyone, and apart from bits remembered from Grantley Dick-Read and the pre-natal breathing classes, I spent all day Thursday wondering what would happen next.

Jim came in when he could get away from work, but as soon as I felt a contraction coming on I asked him to please go. I was much too proud to let him see me screwed up with pain. Eventually, in the very early hours of Friday morning, April 13th, I was wheeled into a brightly lit theatre room. I had just enough time to get a brief glimpse of my doctor, still in his dinner suit with black bow tie, and a few nurses, before a blissful gas mask was popped on my face. I drifted in and out of this vague euphoria, mildly aware of enormous forces clenching the whole of my body, voices, lights… a rushing gushing sensation… and then, a short, sharp, very small human cry. A tiny warm, clammy bundle was put in my exhausted arms, a hot little head nestled under my chin, and I was overwhelmed by the most incredible warm avalanche of powerful, all-consuming maternal love. This little creature that had been growing inside me for those long, miserable, selfishly discontented weeks, this clammy bundle on my shoulder, was my most precious baby daughter, perfect in every cell of her little body, and the first and greatest real and successful personal achievement I had experienced in these first twenty-five years of my life. My joy was overflowing. I no longer noticed the poking and prodding that still seemed to be going on around my tired body. I couldn't wait for Jim to come into the hospital to share my joy, and my pride, to forget the doubts and fears and nausea that had dogged the last eight months, and to show him that all his patience, care and concern for me had really been appreciated; that this so precious little person belonged to us both.

And we called her Janet.

I could not believe how much I adored that little baby girl, after all my doubts. I watched every expression, every movement of her tiny legs and hands, almost every breath she took. I was very lucky in that, after 10 days in the Maternity Hospital, where I only had to worry about Janet at her feeding time, I came home to the full-time help of a Mother Craft Nurse, provided by my mother. Shirley Boundy was amazing, and taught me so much in the care and handling of a new baby, taking so much of the stress, worry and panic out of those first few weeks. She had Janet sleeping in her room, and woke me only for a quick feed when it was necessary. Those sensible and practical lessons helped me to surround my tiny Janet with a sense of calm and security. I think this would still apply today if science, books and endless research had not taken the place of the natural maternal instincts of the birthing mother and introduced so many must's and must not's that seem to keep new parents in a state of minor panic. Janet seemed to love being in her cot and watching the movement of her hands and feet. She didn't need a dummy, but very early in her new life she found the soft edges of her singlet, which, when she held it against her top lip, gave her a comfort that only she could understand, and which seemed to continue to bring her some pensive solace through many decades of her life.

When she was six weeks old I made an excited phone call to Jim in his office:

"What's the matter? What's wrong?" came his worried voice.

"Janet just smiled, a real, proper smile. She smiled right *at* me!"

"Oh—OK. That's nice. Look, I'm a bit busy right now. I'll be a bit late home tonight."

But she had smiled, just for me. I was important to her. I mattered!

Two years and two months later we brought home to our very own, very old, slightly crumbly house in Brunswick Street, Walkerville, a roly-poly eight and a quarter pound baby boy, with big dark brown eyes. This was Richard. I thought I had never seen anything so beautiful, although photos of his infancy show that he may not have won a 'best looking baby' competition! He was such a cuddly baby, but a bit more restless than Janet had been, and very quickly needed some supplement feeding to keep up with his enthusiastic energy.

So we had our 'pigeon pair' and that seemed the right size for our family. But, whoops, three years later, I had somehow got pregnant again and after a day and a half of pushing and puffing along came Tim. He was such a good little undemanding baby and relished the smallest attention that anyone showed him. He just seemed to *fit in* wherever he was plonked.

Life had become extremely busy. Jim's professional life was intensifying and included Saturday morning work and the occasional trip to a country courthouse, involving several days away from home. My life had become a bit of a treadmill – Janet in kindergarten, Richard an energetic and curious toddler, and a new baby to take with me wherever I went.

My mother had died and my father re-married quite soon after her death. My sister-in-law had also died, of cancer, at the age of thirty-six, leaving two young daughters to cope with the early re-marriage of my brother Keith, their father. Life seemed to be one constant state of chaotic exhaustion. Granny Muirhead, Jim's mother, was the only help I could turn to. She was kind and generous with her time and support, although she was in a constant state of bewilderment at the appallingly careless standards of her daughter-in-law's house-keeping.

"Well, at least you keep the children's faces and hands clean, Margaret," was probably the kindest thing she ever said to me. Poor Kitty. Her house was always spotless. The fireplace clean, the veranda swept and the copper in the laundry enthusiastically boiling before 7.00 am, when a large cooked breakfast was all ready and calmly set on the table. Having her only child, who had miraculously survived the jungles, slush and horrors of the War in the Pacific Islands, marry a woman who had *no interest whatsoever* in dusting furniture *every* day, was a cruel blow to this gentle hard-working woman. But her loyal support of me, her generous offers of babysitting, her annual reminder to Jim:

"It's your wedding anniversary next Friday, dear. Are you going to take Margaret out to dinner? The children can come to me and they can stay all night," never faltered.

Other young mothers like me often complained of their mother-in-law's 'interference' in their household responsibilities… '*She actually irons John's shirts when she comes to visit.*'

I relished it. Granny would gather up Jim's shirts when she visited our house, and take them to her steaming copper, '*just to give them a good boil, dear,*' (she totally disapproved of the electric washing machine that my parents had given us as a wedding present), and the shirts would be returned the next day, snowy-white, collars starched, and all beautifully ironed and folded. How could I resent that sort of service?

LOSING MUM

My Mother's death came after a four year period of strokes, alarmingly high blood-pressure and determined rehabilitation. Her first stroke hit her in 1952 when she was 58 years old. I was just 26. My Father called Dr Goode at once and, rightly or wrongly, he decided to treat her by bleeding her! She then had a massive stroke which completely paralysed her down one side of her body, hospitalised her and made her very sick indeed.

My Mother had amazing determination, and was fortunate to have wonderful encouragement from Lib Ross, a physiotherapist and one of Mum's many young friends. With a sweet lisp Lib would urge her patient,

"Come on Mithuth Fwayne, you _can_ do it, pleath twy again."

Gradually and laboriously, with daily visits from Lib, Mum's mobility returned. Her movements and actions were slower, gentler and her attitude to physical frailties had changed completely.

The amazing outcome of this devastating illness of my Mother was that, for some unknown reason, she turned to me as her support and companion. After all those years of feeling that I never quite came up to her expectations, or succeeded in her eyes in anything that I attempted, (except marrying a lawyer, whom she adored), I was now the person who she really enjoyed being with, relying on me for the help that she needed in her slow recovery between each stroke. When the women of her beloved CWA (Country Women's Association) offered Life Membership to her she was delighted, but totally overwhelmed at the thought of the presentation and having to publicly receive this honour. When I tentatively suggested that I could, perhaps, make the 'thank you' speech for her, her appreciation was enormous. I wonder if she ever knew how terrified I was at making my second ever public speech. And I am sure she could not have possibly known the warmth and pride that I felt at so openly being *needed* by my Mother.

These last few years of my Mother's life, I am sure, made the difference between me continuing to be a slightly resentful and embittered person as the supernumerary fourth child, and learning to become a young woman with the knowledge that she had formed a valuable and supportive connection with her mother. And maybe it also sowed the seed that I had some hidden ability to be useful to other unknown people somewhere in the future.

MORE BABIES

So by the time Janet was ten, Richard eight and Tim five, life was starting to level out for me a bit, when Whoops, somehow I was pregnant again.

On July 27th 1961, equally unexpected, but equally as perfect as were the previous three, our fourth, and last, baby was born, although his arrival was preceded by false contractions taking me and my enormous tummy, and even more enormous suitcase, into the Memorial Hospital. The usual enema, shaving, poking and prodding were carried out and then a night of mild discomfort and a wonderful deep sleep from which I awoke the next morning… unfortunately to the same enormous tummy and NO BABY!!!

And so I was sent home to be greeted by three small, very disappointed faces, which prompted the production of a wonderful illustration that Richard had drawn of me lying in an iron bed, a mini-mountain poking up the bedclothes, and a chamber pot conveniently under the bed, presumably to catch the baby when it popped out.

'Mummy Waiting for Baby' by R. Muirhead was a special drawing that I kept for many years.

A week later, after attending the Law Society Dinner Dance with Jim, me dressed in a voluminous black satin coat, my suitcase still on the back seat of the car, I had to face up to the Hospital desk again. This time for real! Except that again, after the usual unpleasant procedures… everything stopped…. Oh no! (Maybe the little baby had had a bit of a preview of the noisy, slightly chaotic family he was about to be launched into and had decided… 'not for me, thanks'.)

But this time they weren't sending me home. Medical inductions, consisting of a series of three injections at separate intervals, were performed *three times*, interspersed with three more enemas!! More poking and prodding, and finally a surgical induction. There was no going back now!

And at last! A rather worn out 34 year old mother was joined by her third absolutely delicious baby boy. A huge sigh of relief all round, and I settled back into the luxury of ten days in hospital, meals and baby delivered to my bed three or four times a day and no cooking, shopping, washing, cleaning or even mopping. The highlights of my day were visits by a busy husband and occasional visits by three wide-eyed children who were allowed no closer to me than the veranda door of my room for their first glimpse of their new baby brother, William Frayne Muirhead.

So all this kept me reasonably happy in hospital, while a young and efficient, Wanslea-trained family-care girl kept Jim and the children very happy at home.

And life should have proceeded peacefully from then on.

A DARKENING WORLD

But, unfortunately, the World had been living under the tensions of the Cold War for some years, and it seemed to be culminating in something horrific in the area of the Caribbean Sea. This was the silent, but seeming stale-mate stand-off between America and the Western democratic world, and Russia and the Communist world.

Tensions had been growing between Russia's assertive 'peaceful competition' and the resultant pressure on the United States, through its President, John F Kennedy, to be 'tough on Russia'. These competing factors included the race into space travel, but, much more unsettling was the arms race and the testing and development of nuclear missiles. By September 1961, after the attempt by Cuban exiles (allegedly backed by the CIA of America), to invade Cuba had failed miserably, Fidel Castro, the leader of Cuba asked for, and was promised by Russia, weapons to defend Cuba against America.

Tensions across the world were immense. We all remembered the hideous results and the questionable ethics of the two nuclear bombs that were dropped on Hiroshima and Nagasaki in Japan in August 1945. This had been an horrendous act of slaughter and mass destruction that brought World War II in the Pacific to a sudden end. But it had been considered by the West to be the only way to bring those past six years of bloodshed and inhumane destruction to an end. So the thought of this same conflagration happening in the world brought a cold clutch of fear to many of our hearts and minds. And in fact, later we read that, '*It was the time when the world came nearest to annihilating itself.*'

For me, with a small baby and three precious lively children to nurture and protect, the fear became almost totally physical. My milk dried up as soon as I left the isolated security of the hospital where the situation had not been helped by a young English nurse whose husband was in the Merchant Navy and was based in the Caribbean Sea. She would come into my room, looking on me as a friendly auntie figure, to off-load her fears of what may be happening to her husband, while I had constant nightmares of fleeing the threatening holocaust to take my helpless little baby to a desert cave in the Centre of Australia.

Meanwhile, the tension between America and Russia mounted frighteningly. Russia was building nuclear missile bases in Cuba, sited within striking distance of North America, and Russian ships carrying missiles were heading for Cuba. John Kennedy, the youngest person to be elected as President of the United States, had the biggest world crisis ever experienced on his hands. On 14 October 1962 Kennedy was told that the Cuban missile bases would be operational in 10 days. He then ordered a naval blockade of Cuba to keep the Russian ships away, and sent B52 nuclear bombers to hover constantly over the whole area surrounding Cuba.

The world held its breath. It was in Kennedy's power to activate the button that would start his planes delivering their disastrous bombs in the Cuban area, and would activate the missiles in the bases that America had set up in Turkey and wherever else America may have built them. But unknown to the world at that time, Kennedy and Khruschev, the Russian leader, were at last starting to negotiate towards a solution to this ghastly nuclear crisis.

Eventually, on 28 October the leaders agreed that Russia would dismantle its Cuban missile bases and America would lift its blockade of Cuba, *and*, a secret agreement at that time, America would also dismantle her missile bases in Turkey which were uncomfortably within striking range of Russia.

The Cuban Crisis was over.

Khruschev later said, '*They talk about who won and who lost. Human reason won… Mankind won*'.

And Kennedy had also said earlier, "*Mankind must put an end to war, or war will put an end to mankind*".

Perhaps we were fortunate that those two men were the world leaders at that time.

But even though the world crisis was over, my own lurking problem of obsessive anxiety eventually and quite suddenly came to a head.

I was very aware that since the birth of our fourth child, 'William but always called Bill,' I had never really regained my energy, and was finding that every day was a bit of a struggle. Added to this feeling of exhaustion, my father died during those months, after a short illness, leaving me feeling strangely bereft and a bit forlorn.

This feeling was not eased as Dad's widow, his second wife Mona, treated our family rather distantly and almost as if we were an impediment to her getting her full share of the inheritance that she expected to receive from him.

So eventually I visited our GP, Dr Arthur Goode, who had been my family's doctor for many years. He decided to take my blood pressure. Normally fairly unflappable, his eyebrows shot up and he said:

"Goodness me! Your blood pressure is very high. Now, let me see. Your mother had very high blood pressure didn't she? And she died quite young. Well, we'll have to watch this. Now, go home and take it easy."

Well, that was not a particularly cheering diagnosis to make to a middle-aged mother-of-four who had been silently stressing for 15 months over the very real possibility that her world and her young family were on the verge of becoming nuclear ash. The next morning when I got out of bed I felt distinctly queer. I went to have a shower and found that I was gasping for breath, my hands were curling up into fists and I couldn't feel my feet. Jim led me back to bed and immediately called our doctor. He came quite quickly, looked very worried and sent me straight to the hospital. Dear Granny Muirhead dropped everything and came at once to manage the household. X-Rays of my head and spine were taken, although I was positive that my end had come. After all, my sister-in-law had died aged 36, leaving two little girls to cope with their father's early re-marriage to a very young woman. Why shouldn't the same thing happen to me?

But Dr Goode could find nothing amiss with me.

The next night, still in hospital, the gasping breathlessness and curled up fingers and toes overcame me again. Being Saturday it was impossible to locate our doctor, (another of those parties), and the nurses 'couldn't possibly disturb any other doctor without Dr Goode's authority'.

Poor Jim, in desperation, rang his cousin John Muirhead, an anaesthetist, and begged him to come to the hospital.

John came quickly, and took one look at me puffing and panting in great distress. Then he firmly but gently held my hand and said in his warm, quiet voice:

"Margie, unless you have an apple stuck in your throat there is no reason at all why you should be breathing like that. Now easy slow breaths please".

I gazed at him as if mesmerised, my breathing settled down and the paralysing tingles gradually disappeared.

And so it was decided that I had had 'a bit of a panic attack, brought on by a bit of tension and depression from being a bit overtired'. And I was sent home. But that was the start of a long battle with tiredness, headaches, listlessness and sometimes valiantly concealed panic attacks. The whole family suffered, and I had no idea how to cope with it all. I was convinced, for many years, that I was constantly on the verge of a stroke that would probably lead to my death -- like my mother. Poor Jim had a very gloomy and boring wife to come home to. Janet, at the age of ten, had been a wonderful second mother to her baby brother Bill. She would come home from school each day, looking at me carefully and say:

"Have you got a headache today Mum? I'll just take Bill for a walk in his pusher".

Poor sweet child. What a worry I was to her.

Eventually I was sent to consult a physician, Dr Britten-Jones. His diagnosis?

"You have what we call cyclical depression. You will be on anti-depressants for the rest of your life"!

What a sentence for a 36 year old woman!

I left his consulting rooms on North Terrace in a daze. But once out on the street I said, almost out loud:

"No way! That is NOT going to happen!"… and I went in to the clothing section of the big Myers store and bought myself the lairiest, most brightly coloured shirt and trousers that I could find. And it did help a lot. But unfortunately depression does not just go away overnight, and there were many times when I uselessly wasted time at home draped across our bed, waiting for some miserable end to it all, only dragging myself into action when the three older children brought themselves home from school.

OUT OF THE DARKNESS

Life at home must have been very trying for Jim and Janet, and probably the three boys as well. I did realise that I needed a break from the treadmill of domestic family life. So I responded to a call for volunteers to help in a new project of a crèche for heavily handicapped pre-school children, an initiative of Dr Helen Heseltine who was only too aware that no such facility existed in Adelaide. After a very brief interview she accepted me willingly, which was a huge surprise and morale booster to me. So one day each week I left Bill at home with 'Barnie', a funny little woman who arrived at 7.00 am wearing what looked like a tea cosy on her head, and who took over the house and the baby for a whole day, even preparing our evening meal for us. I spent the day in the large old rambling house in which the crèche had been set up, simply helping to keep these poor little seriously intellectually handicapped children happy, fed and clean. It amazed me to see how reluctant the parents were to relinquish their children to us, even though it meant that they had a few hours respite to be normal free adults without the ever present burden of the demands of a disturbed child. It was so good for me. How could I really complain that my life created such unpleasant problems for me when I had four intellectually and physically well developed and healthy children at home? I started to see outside my tiny, self-interested world. And, added to that, I was doing something that felt useful.

I also enrolled in Italian classes, having to do homework, and sit for school level exams. The classes were challenging and fun, and my results told me that I still had a brain that could function reasonably well when tested.

But still it wasn't enough. I still wasn't a bundle of joy to live with. I was not a responsive wife. I totally feared another pregnancy, having thrown up or been unwell for most of the nine months of each previous pregnancy, and the contraception of the day did not offer a lot of confidence. The Pill was still new, pretty strong and had warnings that it could cause blood clots. So of course I refused to use it.

In desperation Jim and I agreed that I would consult a friend of ours who was a psychiatrist. This felt to me to be such a 'shame job'. Did this really mean that I had actually become a 'nut case'? In my family there had never been much sympathy for simply feeling a 'bit low'. It was always a matter of 'just snap out of it. You'll be OK.'

But after only a few sessions visiting John Litt he seemed to have total understanding of my fears and frustrations. He encouraged me to talk about the most trivial things in my daily life, a luxury I had not experienced before. He clearly stated that my 'work' at home was equally as important as Jim's, and I felt amazingly relaxed about telling him anything that came into my mind. He would not prescribe for me any mind managing drugs, and at no time did he suggest that my problems were simply self-indulgence and something to just 'forget about'.

Eventually he came up with his solution for my condition.

"Margie," he said, "you bottle up all your emotions. You don't share your problems with Jim, because, you say, his work is so demanding and important that your thoughts and fears are not worth talking about. The only time that you sometimes are able to let go completely is when you have sex. But you are afraid of another pregnancy as you now have four healthy children who keep you more than busy, so that even sex is not an easy outlet for you. You definitely don't want more children?"

"No, not under any circumstances."

"Then, I am recommending that you should be sterilised"!!!!

'Oh, shock!. Oh horror! Oh what would Granny Muirhead say about such a shocking thing?....Oh... wait a minute... Oh my goodness... Oh... golly gosh...Ooooh...What a wonderful idea!!!'

I flew into Jim's office. "Guess what?" and I told him the news. Surprisingly he didn't think it was such a great idea, but eventually I guess he thought anything was better than the half-wife that he had been living with for the past three years.

And so the deed was done... a fairly major operation in those days, with eight days in a small, private hospital. Again, Jim had to cope with a young family, with the help of his wonderful mother, who dropped everything to be available for her grandchildren, and who, a little to my surprise, was not at all shocked at her daughter-in-law having this radical (for the times) surgery. Maybe four children for her to help with were about enough for her too.

So yes, my attitude to my life did improve enormously. One thing that was privately very encouraging to me, was that I had actually survived the operation without having a heart attack or even any sign of a stroke. Perhaps I wasn't on the verge of death after all. Gradually I developed strategies to cope with the times of panic and hyperventilation that would unexpectedly overwhelm me. I found that baking a cake, sewing clothes for the kids, or playing the piano could get me back onto an even keel. But I still felt, more often than was comfortable, that I had to just lie on the bed in a sweaty panic, awaiting the inevitable stroke that was to carry me away from my beloved children for ever, leaving them to the rather regimented, though certainly very caring, life style that Granny and Jim would impose on them.

FAMILY LIFE

But we muddled on as a family.

Jim was more and more involved in his work and his 'after-work drinks' with mates and colleagues. I struggled with the cooking, washing, sewing, not too much housework, and the general treadmill of school lunches, homework, sibling quarrels, music and ballet lessons and kids' friends visiting our house after school. We had acquired two exciting new additions to our home. Three, actually.

The first addition was a television set, a real novelty in 1962. This meant that the kids were sometimes blissfully quiet as they absorbed the Mickey Mouse Club Show, Superman, Roy Rogers & the Cisco kid, though tensions and noise increased when I had to police the amount of time in front of 'the box', otherwise homework never got done.

The second addition to family life was a swimming pool, a very mixed blessing to me. The neighbourhood kids loved it, and there were huge gatherings every afternoon in the summer months. Unfortunately Bill was just five when it was finished, and although he could just keep himself afloat, none of his friends had any idea of how to swim. So I was in constant stand-by mode when he had friends in after school.

But one cold, wintry day when I was doing a load of ironing in the laundry overlooking the pool, and Bill and a little friend were playing outside, I suddenly heard a wild yell:

"Mum! Mum!"

It didn't sound good.

I raced outside, down the steps, and saw Bill looking into the deep end of the pool where his little friend, Henry Rymill, was floundering in the water about two feet below the surface of the pool, getting further and further from the edge. I was wearing a heavy winter skirt, solid shoes, thick jumper and a brand new hair-do in readiness for a dinner that Jim and I were going to that night. With one leap I was in the eight feet of freezing water, boots and all, grabbed Henry by the back of his jumper and with strength that I had no idea that I possessed, heaved him up and over the parapet of the pool, and with one easy jump, bounded up after him myself, with surprising alacrity.

Bill was struck dumb with alarm. He had no idea that anyone in the water couldn't just paddle their way out again. He also looked suitably guilty. It seemed that he had been waving the long handled leaf-skimmer around, and inadvertently caught Henry off-balance and tipped him into the pool. A soggy, highly embarrassed me, and a rather subdued young Bill returned the shivering Henry home to his mother who was wonderfully un-derstanding and reassuring to us both.

My reaction to this rather startling experience was to organise weekly swimming classes for all the children in Bill's kindergarten, and these became quite friendly and happy occasions, and thank-fully, there were no more episodes of small children floundering in the deep end of our pool.

Our third new acquisition was a most beautiful four month old Samoyed puppy, passed on to us by friends who had found her 'too much bother to cope with'. She was snow white with black rims around her large brown eyes, a black nose, and a joyful and mischievous personality. We all fell in love with her on the spot, although Granny Muirhead said, 'you can't possibly have a dog *and* a small child in the same house!'

The dog's name was 'Kista Antarctic Morn' and she was im-mediately a very important member of the family. Rather than being a problem with a baby, Kista took on the responsibility of being Bill's minder. When he was in the sand pit she would place herself on the ground beside him. Outside in the pram, she would again post herself on guard by the pram. When a neighbour looked after Bill for a few hours one afternoon, Kista would not let her go near him in the pram, even to change his nappy. Coming out of the bath, drippy wet, Bill would nonchalantly pick up Kista's fluffy white tail to wipe himself dry. She seemed happy to think that that was part of her duties as well.

Of course, Kista wasn't always perfect. Neighbour's ducks and chooks got slaughtered; the sheep in the paddock opposite our house were given good exercise by Kista chasing them, prompting Mr Webster, the owner, to wave his gun threateningly at her, much to the kids' horror. Her worst ever act was that, early one Christmas morning, she broke into the birdcage that housed quite a number of the boys' budgerigars, ripping down their nests and killing every one of their newborn chicks. That was not a happy Christmas, but she managed to remain totally adored by all of us.

JUST THE WIFE

So now the year is 1966.

Janet was 15 and attending the Wilderness School, my old school. Richard at 13 was in the Senior School at Pulteney Grammar School. Tim, aged 10 was now in the Prep School at Pulteney Grammar, and Bill at five had, a little reluctantly the year before, started his schooling at St Andrews Kindergarten. Bill was a delightfully quiet, self-contained little boy, and although he was very excited about going to school, on Day One he was amazed to discover that it wasn't just a one-off experience... school was there *forever!*

After that first day, it took quite some time before he could see any good reason to go off to school, even though it was only for the morning. Often there were quiet little tears as I dropped him off with Miss Pearce, his tall thin pale-faced kindergarten teacher. One morning I asked her if he settled as soon as I was out of sight.

"Weeeeelll," she said carefully, "he usually stops crying by recess time. Often I just carry him around with me for the morning".

Poor little Bill. It made me feel like a monster mother.

So there were virtually four different schools and all their different time-tables to contend with. Four school fêtes to bake for, four tuck shops to help with, four Speech Days, Sports Days, end-of-year school plays and Carol Nights, parents' nights and fund-raisers to attend throughout the year. And of course, football matches, rowing regattas, basketball games, school dances, ballet performances, music lessons, birthday parties—all had to be juggled and attended, driven to, collected from—with everyday family life slotted in somewhere amongst all the flurry, arguments and excitement.

They were hectic days, but occasionally Jim and I would have a night out on our own so that we would have adult time together. Again Jim's mother came forward with help. She would ring Jim and say:

"Jim dear, you haven't taken Margaret out to dinner for a while. I can have the children on Friday night, and they can stay all night if you like. Just pick them up on Saturday when you are ready."

Those were blissful times, and even though the table talk was always about Jim's work it made me feel a little included in his life and helped me to learn a bit about the Law, and to not feel quite so intellectually useless. And of course, it was so good to have the rest of the night at home on our own without having to face a talkative babysitter, or get up in the early hours of the morning to a restless child.

Life was starting to feel much better.

Another social change that occurred in the '60's and brought with it some interesting developments, was the introduction of the contraception medication for women, simply referred to as *The Pill*. This seemed to bring with it a new level of freedom and fun at many of our dinner parties. After the Kinsey Report which recorded surprisingly frank and rather alarming results from the research of Masters and Johnson into the sexual behaviour between men and women in the late 50's and early 60's, the topic of *S.E.X.* became an open subject for dinner party discussions, as had religion a few years earlier, after Billy Graham had conducted many of his crusades all over the Western world. Both of these subjects had been very much 'taboo' at the 'acceptable' middle-class gatherings and dinner parties, such as those we went to and held in Walkerville and in the better foothills suburbs of Adelaide. But now the conversation became much more stimulating and lively, and women were starting to join in the discussions and making their voices heard a little more than in past years when a wife, as a general thing, simply agreed with whatever her husband was talking about, in the accepted model of obedience. The parties of the sixties often went on till the early hours of the morning, lots of jokes and innuendos went on between the couples who were present at these gatherings, and the evenings usually finished with dancing in dim-lit rooms, seldom with your own partner, and often with very suggestive words and actions shared, and also concealed, in the darkened shadows of the lounge room of the host's home, or in their swimming pool if the weather was right. These parties were fun, titillating and usually totally inconse-quential, and most of us went home, keyed up a little and excited by the outside attention that we had received, or been able to give, and consequently perhaps, with a little more *zing* in our attention to our own partners. Whatever, in most cases no harm was done.

However, there were some groups, we understood, who had 'key parties'. Each man threw the keys of his car into a bowl and each wife took a set of keys at random. This meant that you went home with the man whose keys you had selected. *Veerrry* risky, most of us thought, but we were assured that it happened amongst the *nicest* of people. This new sense of freedom all seemed to come about with the new-found opening up of the ability to talk more freely about a previously and rigidly unspoken subject… *sex*. The introduction of The Pill certainly earned that era the heading of 'The Swinging Sixties.'

1966 was also the year that decimal currency was introduced into Australia. Many older people were not happy at having to give up the Pound for the Dollar…' *much too American! If we have to have new currency it should be called The Royal!*', and most of us felt that somehow we were not getting our full value as 10 cents was now equal to a shilling when before it had been 12 pennies to the shilling. But of course, school arithmetic was much easier to cope with as everything was now in multiples of ten. And like any change, we gradually got used to all these funny little 1 cent and 2 cent coins that were rattling around in our purses.

And early in the next year Jim's first major professional success was announced. He was invited by the Chief Justice of the Supreme Court of South Australia to 'take Silk', that is, to become a Queen's Counsel, a senior member of the Bar. At that time in South Australia lawyers did not apply to become Silks as in most of the other States. It was purely on the recommendation of the Judges, with advice from the Law Society, that such a position was granted. In this year of 1967 only two lawyers, Jim and Len King, were appointed, both of them only forty-two years old. It was a huge honour and a great acknowledgement of Jim's legal ability and integrity. We were all very excited, and Jim was endearingly overwhelmed by the fuss that was made of him, with phone calls of congratulations coming in all through the evening, a little to the frustration of one hungry teen-age boy who had to wait ages for his dinner.

The next year was not so cheery as that was when the kids' beloved Granny, their one remaining grandparent, developed cancer of the pelvis. With her usual stoicism she spent several weeks in hospital, accepting whatever treatment was available to her at that time. But when there was not a lot more that the doctors could do for her other than keep her as comfortable as possible, she begged Jim to let her go home so that she could at least see her beloved garden through her bedroom window.

With the help of one of Jim's many cousins he was able to arrange around-the- clock nursing care for Kitty. Her doctor kept her well supplied with morphine and 'happy drugs' and she spent a couple of relatively pain-free months in her own home, enjoying the 'young and pretty' nurses who spent every hour of the day and night taking care of her. Jim called in every evening after work and sat with her for an hour or two, also enjoying the company of the nurses! Granny chose not to have other visitors, especially her grandchildren as she did not want them to see her so frail and depleted, and she quietly died in the peace of her home of many years, at Number 6 Arthur Street Medindie.

Perhaps by design and to be sure that her son would always remember it, she died on February 4th 1968, the 18th anniversary of our Wedding Day.

It was so sad for all of us that we no longer had Kitty as part of our family, but selfishly, and secretly, I rejoiced in the fact that Jim would come home after work now, and would be able to spend more time with us and resume his role of husband and father.

But alas, this was not to be the case for several more months as he found himself caught up in a triangular situation within his law firm. It seemed that two young women connected with the office were vying for the same man……. One woman, an attractive and highly intelligent, black-stockinged new Law graduate, was Jim's articled clerk, and the other was the wife of one of his younger partners. It was the latter's husband who was the 'piggy-in-the-middle' for the two women. For some reason Jim felt duty bound to counsel both women, separately of course, and seemingly at length. Of course, as it all seemed to be part of The Job, the kids and I just got on with life as usual, eating our evening meals in relative peace, but with a certain lack of excitement that always seemed to be a part of Jim's presence.

My favourite times of these years were always the school holidays. We were so lucky to have the choice of beach or hills for holidays. We still had the Block at Aldgate with its very primitive but much loved, almost camping accommodation, and added to that, with one of his partners, Bill Ross, Jim had bought a house at Sellicks Beach.

This house was about 40 miles south of Adelaide, a simple three bedroomed cottage set high up on a cliff overlooking the wonderful long white expanse of Sellicks Beach. In the summer we went to Sellicks, and in the winter to the Aldgate Shack. Jim would help transport the children, always with two or three of their friends, plus food, luggage, dog, surfing, fishing and beach equipment; or racquets and blankets, matches and candles, depending on the season. Once he had settled us all in to our holiday spot he would go back to the Walkerville house for his work, sometimes joining us on weekends. There seemed to be an amazing feeling of almost total freedom for these special weeks.

All the children, visitors included, accepted that there was a roster for the washing up and drying dishes, wood collecting and fire making. We played 'Racing Patience' and other card games at all hours of the day. The bigger kids seemed to keep an eye on the smaller ones, and for most of the time we seemed to be one big happy mob.

With the arrival of Jim on the weekends we all had to tidy up our living standards a bit, make beds, wash up after each meal etc. but it also brought more exciting activities for the kids as Jim was able to organise much more adventurous things for them to do; driving lessons on the beach, or on the Block at Aldgate, fishing trips and hair-raising rides on a tyre dragged behind the car on the flat hard sands of Sellicks Beach; long hikes through the blackberries and creeks of Aldgate, and, of course, usually the pre-lights-off story that Jim often told them, making it up out of his very fertile mind as he went along.

And so our family life in Adelaide settled into a fairly regular pattern; University for Janet, Technical School for Richard, Senior School for Tim and Primary School at Saint Peter's College for Bill. Janet kept us on our toes by moving in, and out, of group housing with various girl-friends. But when she was at home she kept the air well-stirred by demanding honest answers to challenging questions about God, Sex and Communism.

Richard kept us equally nervously on our toes with motor-bikes, surfing, girls, very long hair and very loud music of songs that, surprisingly, had deep, political messages.

Tim went very quietly about his life… school, football, friends, a bit of theatre acting and a lot of thinking. Bill was timidly quiet most of the time, but secretly adored by all the family.

And I got on with the household chores, always with a cleaning lady, usually Italian, a bit of gardening, lots of sewing, occasional games of tennis and Bridge, attendance at school functions and driving support and occasional meals for Jim's many aunts.

SECTION 4
NEW HORIZONS

A WIDENING WORLD

Then, in 1970, Jim decided it was time that he and I did an overseas trip. With the sale of his mother's house he was able to pay off the perennial bank overdraft that had dogged us all our married life, and also to pay off his tax, which was always hovering over him. And, surprisingly, he found there was a small amount left over to pay for travel. The Travel Agent told us we could get a very good rate if we were away for 60 days. So that was it!! Two months away from work, family, domestic chores and suburban sameness. Poor kids!! I don't think we thought it through from their points of view. A Wanslea girl for the first few weeks and then my cousin, Marie, and her rather fearsome husband and their four children came from the country to look after our probably very resentful young family.

But off we went.

I was so excited. My first time out of Australia; Mauritius was my first step on foreign soil, and from then on I seemed to be two feet off the ground as, after five fascinating days in Mauritius we moved on to South Africa, Kruger Park, then London, Buckingham Palace, Big Ben, the magical ballet of 'Giselle' at Covent Gardens, the colourful opera of 'Carmen' at another great West End theatre; Amsterdam, Germany, 'Sound of Music' country, the dancing horses of Vienna, mountains, snow, cable-cars, gondolas, the Colosseum… All magic.

Of course there were minor problems on the way, and irritable tiredness occasionally came in to it. One major event that had us both terrified though was when the wheels of the plane carrying us from Johannesburg to London refused to come down into landing position. The pilot calmly announced that we would fly on to another airport where there was "better..er… landing equipment." (*oh yes, thought I, he means better hospitals and ambulances and things*), and he proceeded to duck and dive in this huge flying machine in an effort to shake the wheels down. After two hours of flying through darkness there was one almighty shudder and the weary voice of the pilot came across on the intercom:

"Ladies and gentlemen, you will be pleased to know that our wheels are now firmly in place and in ten minutes we will make a perfect landing at Isle da Sol."

Oh my hat. That really was a very horrible experience.

We finished this extended overseas trip of ours with a couple of shopping-filled days in Hong Kong, a perfect place to buy compensatory presents for the kids, (and some beautiful pearls for me). Then home at last.

And in spite of our long absence all seemed fine at home… Richard had almost written off our Mazda station wagon, loaded with 7 or 8 of his hefty rugby mates, and Janet had almost written off 13 year old Tim by somehow persuading him to drink half a flagon of sherry. Bill, at nine, seemed unscathed, and his usual placid, angelic little self.

So – back to normal Walkerville life again. But then, soon after our return from The Big Trip the next bit of excitement came along. Jim received a phone call from Neil Ligertwood, the Chief Judge of the new South Australian District and Criminal Court, asking him if he would consider becoming one of the six Judges in that Court.

Jim was delighted. The Queen's Counsel work that he had been doing for the past three years had not excited him much. With no direct contact with his client, as is the norm for Senior Counsel, he missed the personal, face to face consultations that he had always enjoyed and was so good at. He was still based in private practice in the law firm of Thomson and Co. but always had to act through a solicitor who would give him the instructions on behalf of the client. But this new promotion to 'The Bench', working for the South Australian Government, meant financial security, an assured retirement superannuation pension and possibly more regular working hours. We were all happy.

After all the ups and downs, joys and dramas of twenty years of married life, we all seemed to be growing into our individual ways of living constructively, all occupied in our separate ways, but still closely united, and a reasonably well-functioning family.

At about the same time, largely due to Janet talking to the mother of her babysitting job, I was asked to do some part-time work with Theodore Bruce, an up-market auctioneering firm. My cousin Marie also worked there and it was interesting and quite fun work... *and* it paid me a little bit of money, *all my own*! This job didn't require a huge amount of expertise, but widened my world quite a bit. The first project for me was assisting in the sorting and cataloguing of the most extensive library of Charles R J Glover, a gentleman who lived in Adelaide and who, in 1919, became the first Lord Mayor of Adelaide. The library was a collection of nearly 3,000 books and maps of Australiana, and included many books on New Zealand, New Guinea and early comments on Australian Aboriginal people and their cultures. It was 'housed in the magnificent library of the Glover family home, St Andrews, on Kingston Terrace, Adelaide,' and the books lined every wall, from floor to ceiling, in that imposing room.

So it was here that Babilly Bruce, the wife of the Auctioneer, and I sat for many days finalising the 290 page catalogue which contains every one of those books.

Shell collections, fine china, and the total contents of the South Australian Hotel, the most prestigious hotel of old Adelaide, were also areas in which I found myself following Babilly's in-structions, and trying to look suitably knowledgeable. But in fact, my knowledge of fine china, crystal and the more highly valued trappings of Adelaide Society was abysmal. At one sale of fine antique furniture and delicate china, a potential purchaser came to me and asked to see the *'mice and things'*. I, with my head still half submerged in children's hobbies, pets and school functions, went to Babilly and said to her,

"That woman would like to see the white mice wherever they are?"

Babilly looked at me with her charming and attractive smile, puzzled at first and then with a slight look of disbelief at my total crassness, said,

"Oh, that is the *Meissen* China. It is very delicate porcelain first created in the early 18th Century near Dresden. It is in the drawing room in the far corner."

So it was all a very good experience for me, and lifted me a little way out of the domestic treadmill that seemed to have become my *norm*.

PAPUA NEW GUINEA

Then one day, early in 1971, as Marie and I were sorting the crystal and porcelain for the next auction sale, Jim came into the auction house to tell me that he had been asked to go to Papua New Guinea for five months to take the place of a Supreme Court Judge who was going on long service leave. And he was needed there next week!!

Oh dear, and life was just starting to go so smoothly.

We all went with him to the Adelaide Airport to see him off on this new adventure in that strange and primitive land where, as a very young 19 year old he had endured the shocking 'coming of age' experience of battling a hidden and determined enemy, hampered by the mud, mosquitoes, diseases and tragedies of the jungles of Papua New Guinea and its Islands.

I remember well his strangely prophetic parting words as he left us all at the departure gate to walk across the tarmac to the waiting plane…

"Here starts the flying era…"

So, yet again, the kids and I settled back into life without Father, and we got into a pretty good routine. With Janet and Richard both having their driving licences now, the to-ing and fro-ing to extra classes, school trips, parties, doctors' appointments, sports matches etc etc was not as onerous as in earlier days, and house rules became comfortably relaxed without Jim's work-wearied eagle eye of disapproval roaming over most home activities.

And then…. an unexpected phone call from Papua New Guinea…

"Darling, this place is just so fascinating. You would find it so interesting up here, and I am missing you terribly. Can you possibly get away from the kids for a couple of weeks and come and travel with me? Please do."

Well of course I could. The adrenalin started rushing giddily through my veins. A few busy phone calls, a long list of instructions to Janet and Richard…

"Of course we can manage, Mum. Bim and John and the Twinnies are just next door and are always so helpful. Just don't stay too long…"

And I was off on my second ever plane flight on my own. My first stop was Sydney where my sister and her family visited me at the Airport Hotel – although I was so nervous and pent up about what I was doing and what might lie before me that I was barely coherent. I could hardly wait for them to leave so that I could shiver with this enormous apprehension that was gushing over me in great waves, and to just be alone in the emptiness of the huge strange hotel bed.

Flying up the East coast of Australia, in a rattling DC3, fascinated by the coral islands in clear blue and green seas below us, my apprehension still had a tight hold over me. Sitting next to me on the plane was a youngish man who didn't help much. He often travelled to PNG he said, "*only* because I have to. It's a dreadful place," he added.

"Oh, my husband seems to like it," I said in a small voice.

"Nah! Full of sickness. Remember *never* drink the water... don't *ever* have ice in your drinks. You will, for sure, get very sick. Never go out at night, the mosquitoes are laden with malaria, and the natives will be after you anyway. They're all half savage... Cannibals some of them, too... I don't know why Australia bothers with the place."

Oh dear, what was I letting myself in for? My poor children... would I ever see them again?

At last, with a bump or two, we landed at the Port Moresby airstrip. Great tall palm trees leaned giddily on all sides of the alarmingly narrow strip. Quickly through Customs and there was Jim. Such a welcoming smile, such a warm, strong embrace. Such joy.

He introduced me to his smiling, shiny black-faced driver and we were whisked off through the incredible sticky heat of the outside air into a cool car. Tightly holding hands in the back seat as Fragi drove us to the house Jim was living in, we passed through streets lined with colourful tropical trees and bushes, the footpaths dotted with beautiful black-skinned people, dressed in so many different colours, feathers and flowers in their hair and around their wrists. My eyes were popping out, but my main attention was for this man next to me who was taking such a real and obvious delight in having me beside him.

Fragi drove us up a steep winding gravel driveway through a lush and overgrown tropical garden to the wide wooden verandah of a large, low bungalow. A dark skinned man, with large bare feet, wearing a long white wrap-around skirt held in place by a wide red sash, waited for us at the front door.

"This is Sam," said my husband, and Sam bowed to me, lifting his head and showing a huge smile and strangely red-stained teeth. He giggled a bit and disappeared inside, carrying my bags.

"Sam looks after the house, the cooking, the washing, every-thing, *and* us," Jim told me, obviously delighted with Sam. "He chews betel nut all the time, that's why he giggles a bit and his teeth are red. Betel nut is a bit addictive, but it keeps him happy and doesn't seem to do him any harm. He has a lot of his '*wantoks*' come from their villages to stay with him. I think the betel nut helps him to cope with the overcrowding."

"Oh, goodness me" I murmured.

This was certainly a strange new world I had landed in. And so far, the strangest and most wonderful part of this new world was the unflagging delight, warm affection and thoughtfulness that Jim was showering upon *me*.

And for the next amazing five weeks of my stay in PNG that warmth and care never wilted. Jim seemed to take such pride in having me with him. He included me whenever possible in ev-erything that he did. I met all the other Judges and their wives, sat in Courts in remote villages, visited prisons in jungle compounds, wandered through local markets, visited '*kiaps*' (lay Magistrates) and their families and attended official functions in the capital, Port Moresby.

There was so much to see, to absorb and to *learn*. The language, Pidgin English, or '*Tok Pisin*' fascinated me and I learned words whenever I could…'*rot bilong blut*'…a vein,'*rot bilong picaninny*'… vagina, …'*balus belong rot*'… a Jeep, '*tasol*'… that's all, and so on.

The Lord's Prayer, used on the Missions, starts off:

'Papa bilong mipela
Yu stap long heven...'

It is not a difficult language to manage, and I loved listening to it, and trying a few words whenever I could.

In those five weeks, we spent ten days in Lae, a steamy coastal town with lush gardens everywhere and amazingly colourful flowers and orchids growing almost wild. We spent two weeks in the Highlands at Goroka, a week in Wau, a tiny hills town set on a steep sloping hill, and a few days back in Port Moresby with Sam looking after us, usually hiding his giggles behind his long black hand.

We always travelled by plane, the biggest being an unpressurised DC 3 that struggled to gain the altitude necessary to skim over the Owen Stanley Ranges. To get to the little village of Wau we travelled in a very small plane and landed on an alarmingly sloping grassy hill. The landing site was scarily short so the plane flew up-hill as it landed, stopping quite quickly, and then it flew down-hill as it took off to help get up enough speed to be able to get off the ground, over the trees of the dense jungle and into the air. Oh my!... and I thought that the South African flight was the risky one.

In Wau, Jim was hearing a case of alleged murder. His Court House, the local community shelter, was surrounded every day by all the '*wantoks*' of the accused PNG tribesman, some in their traditional mourning dress of white mud and '*billum*' netting. They all just sat quietly on the grass, patiently waiting for the outcome of the strange procedures of this white man's court. Jack, the manager of the local hotel that we were staying in, a rather fat and morose 'ex-pat' from Australia, said to me, gloomily:

"Your husband had better move quickly if he finds that black-fella guilty. All those *wantoks* sitting around won't be quite as quiet then. I reckon there'll be Big Trouble. Do you see all the extra Police they've brought in? I hope there'll be a plane ready for you to make a quick getaway."

It didn't seem to worry Jim at all. Maybe he knew all along that there was not a good case against his poor little defendant and as all cases in PNG were heard by Judge alone, that is, no jury, he could be fairly certain of the outcome, though of course he kept it completely private, even from me.

Some of the problems between ex-pats and the people of PNG were illustrated by an incident later that same evening, when I was dismayed by the attitude of the gloomy manager. After dinner, just three of us were left in the dining room when Jack, the 'ex-pat' manager, addressed the waiter, a '*Buka Boy*' from Bougainville. The 'Boy' was a tall, strongly built man with beautiful shiny blue-black skin and a proud stance. Jack, the manager, proceeded to tell the 'Boy' off, in front of us, for not washing the hotel car at the right time, and also for not feeding the dogs early enough. Not a muscle flickered on the face of this warrior-like man, but his jet-black eyes seemed to glint with red flashes as he had to stand and listen to this abusive tirade, and in front of guests, including the 'big judge' from Australia! It crossed my mind that Jack should give some thought to his own security rather than make pronouncements about the safety of the gentle Judge who loved all these local people so much that he hated to ever have to commit any of them to a prison sentence. After all, many of them were the descendants of those heroic 'Fuzzy Wuzzy Angels' who gave their lives to help the young Australian foot-soldiers who were doing their muddy, jungle-swamped best to eliminate the Japanese invaders from this country. A poem that Jim wrote and which is recorded in his memoirs, 'A Brief Summing Up', gives a little insight into the dislocation suffered by an indigenous offender affected by the sentences that Jim, as the presiding Judge, was bound to hand down.

Goroka was a bigger town set on the edge of the jungle, up in the Highlands. We visited the rather benign and pleasant prison there. It was visiting day which happened quite often. People came in from their villages, often a day's walk, or a couple of day's paddling in a dug-out canoe. They brought fresh fruit and special foods from their own supplies for their incarcerated family member. Prisoners sat with their families, both inside the prison confines and outside it on the grassy slopes. It was an amazingly festive and happy atmosphere. John Purcell, the Comptroller of Prisons in PNG who showed us around, seemed to know quite a few of the families, and their prisoner, all of whom appeared to be rather enjoying the pleasant picnic outing. I think it helped to make Jim's job of sentencing a bit easier.

The Court House was, again, an informal open-air sort of building. Because the offenders came from so many different sur-rounding areas two interpreters were needed for every case, one for translating the '*plase tok*'—the village language—into Pidgin, and then one to translate Pidgin into English. Who knows how many slips of interpretation confused the evidence and changed the direction of the trial, depending on the popularity of the accused. But it certainly elongated each case with its fairly slow pace.

Jim encouraged me to sit in the Court to absorb the atmo-sphere. Of course, this was all fascinating to me, although the body odour was something to get used to. Many of the prisoners, after walking long distances and paddling several creeks to get to the White Man's Court, came in their village dress, a flower or feather in their hair, a tattered shirt and 'arse-grass'. Arse-grass is a sort of grass skirt, concentrated more at the back, the purpose being mainly, I think, to be used as on-site toilet paper. It didn't smell pretty.

When Jim dismissed a witness after the lengthy three language evidence, he would tell him to "Go sit at the back of the court, next to that lady in the dress." I felt his care of me had taken a bit of a mischievous turn.

Goroka was full to bursting with new sights and experiences for me. Again, I had an uncomfortable moment with an 'ex-pat'. She was a very pleasant, attractive young Australian wife who took me to her home before taking me out to lunch. But when she saw her 'boy' hanging the washing on the line she launched into a loud and aggressive lecture *at* him about all the things that he was doing wrong, and the dire consequences if he didn't improve, "*immediately!*" Not pleasant, and I found it a bit hard to fully enjoy her company, although it did swiftly change back to charming, after she had let fly with that ugly outburst.

The local markets of the Highlands were a constant fascination for me. Fruits, nuts, bunches of leaves, meaty bones all laid out on banana leaves on the dirt floor of the market. A beautiful, bare-breasted young girl wearing a necklace of frangipani and a grass skirt, nose painted red and a scarlet hibiscus in her frizzy black hair, shyly posed for a photo with me, and a slightly older woman squatted behind her pile of bananas, a small child suckling from one breast and a slightly smaller piglet suckling from the other. A much older woman sat swatting the flies away from her pile of smoked bones and strips of meat. Her breasts were well past their use-by date and seemed to be stretching almost to the ground. Tribesmen in various dress wandered through the market, some with bones through their noses, or ears, and nearly all of them wearing a flower, feather or piece of grass in their hair.

Further out of town I saw the 'mud men'. Their dress was just green mud, caked all over them. The dense jungle was festooned with unbelievably large hanging bunches of bright red and sea-green flowers, shaped like a cockatoo's beak, and looking almost plastic. It was all breath-taking.

The local *kiap*, Steve Easterbrook, had a 'special treat' for me when we visited his home near a mountain village. Steve was the local Patrol Officer for that area and was responsible for overseeing law and order, sorting out simple differences, with and without police assistance, and sitting in Court hearing minor matters of theft, disputes over 'bride price' and inter-village skirmishes.

While we were meeting his family and enjoying a cup of tea, Steve reached under my chair and pulled out a large sack.

"We found this for you, Margaret, in the Poinciana tree out there," he said to me.

"How sweet," I thought, "some furry little baby animal..."

Wrong! Out came a huge, fat, writhing green and yellow tree snake.

"Oh goodness me," I said as calmly as I could.

Of course, we all had to go outside for photos with this monster draped amongst us. Steve's children just loved it. I think, (I hope), I managed to look relaxed, and may have made one finger rest briefly on the bright green scales of the first snake that I had ever seen!

And so my education of the reality of a bigger, wider, different world from safe and secure little old Adelaide was launched. I thought I had seen it all when we went to Europe... but PNG was *so* different. So many black skinned people, in the villages, in the work place, in the professions, at the University, at our dinner table! My ingrained ideas and values of *'our way is the right and only way'* were being pushed around in a quite alarming manner. Dining in the other Judges' houses, the meal and the settings were similar to life in Australia, but the fuzzy-haired black-skinned people cooking and waiting at table were important in their own right, and they were treated almost as family. Not quite 'equality' but most certainly respect and often affection were demonstrated at all times by the Judge and his wife towards the people who helped them to live a very comfortable life, albeit one rather restricted by local problems and the dynamic weather in this foreign, tropical country.

And all of this was happening to me in the glow and warmth of Jim's constant attention to my well-being, and his continuing pleasure at having me with him in this most exotic country.

So it came as an unwelcome jolt to my enjoyment when a phone call from Janet came one evening. It was a few days before our departure for the island of Bougainville and more exciting experiences which I was really looking forward to.

"Mum," she said very seriously, "we think it is time that you came home."

Oh bother! My heart stopped quite still for a moment. But then, the frisson of guilt that reminded me of the four kids on their own for these five weeks, managed to get the beat started again, and rather swiftly.

Regretfully I packed my tropical luggage, fondly farewelled my attentive husband as he went off to Court that day, and was driven out to the Port Moresby airport by our lovely black driver in our lovely air-conditioned car.

My flight home was a little gloomy, but the welcome that greeted me from four poor neglected children surrounded me with all the warmth and joy that I needed to get me happily back into the domestic life of Number 54 Brunswick Street, Walker-ville. And this time there were no hair-raising stories of alcohol poisoning and car smashes, though more likely the kids had learnt the lesson of 'safety in silence'. However, it did seem that during the 18 months since our trip to Europe a certain amount of responsibility and a shade of maturity had crept into the two older members of our family. And they *did* seem pleased to have me home again.

A couple of months later Jim came home from PNG. It had been a fascinating time for him too. He had visited so many outposts of Papua New Guinea, including the beach and jungle of Bougainville where he had landed as a very young foot-soldier 28 years before, and where he had dug slushy fox-holes and set up signal posts for his sometimes erratic system, searching for the elusive Japanese soldiers in that dense and clammy jungle. He brought home with him, after suitable quarantining, some fascinating souvenirs of his first court cases in Mendi; the bow and arrow used by a disgruntled husband when he killed his wife who had not performed well enough to warrant the large 'bride-price' that he had paid for her; several spears that had been used in a village fight over the theft of pigs, which were almost as valuable as children, and some special artefacts given to him in appreciation of a good outcome of a dispute between two warring clans.

So that was 1971.

LEAVING WALKERVILLE

The year 1972 moved along smoothly. Jim was back in the District and Criminal Court. Janet was into her 3rd year at Flinders University where she was studying for an Arts Degree. She was 21. Richard was in his 2nd year at the Institute of Technology working reasonably well on his Diploma of Town Planning. Tim was in Year 11 at Pulteney Grammar School, and Bill, turning 11, was more or less happily in Year 5 at Jim's old school, Saint Peter's college. I was back to a bit of Bridge, a bit of tennis, some morning-tea parties, an occasional job at the Auction house, and a rather tentative attempt at book-keeping with a mail-order wine merchant. Life was quite mellow, predictable, and maybe a tiny bit boring. Except that my brother, Keith, had developed a galloping cancer that rapidly invaded his whole body, and I had to helplessly watch him suffer, amazingly courageously, and with great fortitude, to an early death at the age of 52.

His second wife, Susie, and their three quite young boys were left to somehow manage on their own.

For the first time in my life of 45 years, I attended a funeral, my brother's. Up until then it seemed to be unacceptable for women to go to graveyard burials. For the deaths of my grandfather, my grandmother, my father-in-law, my mother, my sister-in-law and then my father I had never really been able to fully acknowledge the final closing of their lives because I was not present at that last solemn rite that marked the end of each of their journeys in this world. How much better it was for me to openly accept the death of my brother by actually being there at that final emotional commemoration of his life.

And then, towards the end of 1972, our predictable family suburban lives were given the most startling and unexpected jolt.

Jim had, for several years, been an active and very enthusiastic member of a National community body called the Australian Crime Prevention and Aftercare Council. Members of the Council came from every State and Territory of Australia. They were representatives of the law, police, social workers, prison officers and academics, all actively interested in improving the Criminal Justice system of this country and, in particular, the treatment and rehabilitation of offenders who had received sentences of imprisonment for their crimes. With some regular pressure from this body of people, the Federal Government decided to set up a National Institute of Criminology which would carry out research and education in all areas of the Criminal Justice system of Australia.

To Jim's great excitement, he was invited to take on the job of setting up this Institute, not as a permanent position but for the two or three years that the establishment of such an Institute might take.

Yes, of course it was an exciting idea, and very flattering to a man of 47 years from the small out-of-the-way city of Adelaide, to be invited to create a *National* body in Canberra.

But – as this was a Federal appointment it would be necessary for Jim to live in Canberra to be near the seat of the Government and also to be on site for the creation and development of the new Institute. I was appalled at the idea. But all the kids seemed really excited and said, 'of course Dad must take on this job.' And, of course, Dad 'really wanted to do this job.' And so decisions were quickly made.

Jim had to be in Canberra to start 'the job' on February 1st 1973. Richard and Tim stated categorically that they needed to stay on in Adelaide as each was in his final year of their tertiary and secondary education. Janet decided that she could transfer her Flinders University Arts Degree to the Australian National University and poor young Bill had no choice…. he was going to Canberra and would go to the nearest school, and I…..? Numbly, and with a minimum of enthusiasm, I accepted the inevitable fact that in those days a woman just followed her husband to wherever his work may take him, never mind the losses.

And so, in a few short weeks, the house at 54 Brunswick Street Walkerville, set in its great big tree-filled garden, where we had lived and loved for 20 years, expanding it as needed by our growing family, was quickly auctioned and sold at a much reduced price. A small cottage in Unley was rented for the two older boys to live in, and furniture was dispatched in five separate pantechnicons to five different destinations.

On the morning of January 30th 1973 we set off from Adelaide in two cars to drive to Canberra. Originally, Janet was going to drive one of the cars as I didn't feel confident to drive that long distance on country roads. But unfortunately, or carelessly maybe, Janet woke that morning with a 'tummy wog' brought on, I later learned, by a particularly heavy farewell party the night before. So, young Tim, just turned 16 and with a brand new driving licence, was quickly called in to drive my car. And off we set from my cousin Marie's house where we had stayed for our last night in Adelaide, Janet lying in the back seat of the car that her young brother was nobly driving, her left foot waving drunkenly out of the back window, farewelling her cousins, and our life in Adelaide.

AUSTRALIA'S CAPITAL CITY

Canberra!!! What was this foreign country I had landed in?

We five road-weary travellers were accommodated in the Forrest Motor Inn. Tim flew back to Adelaide, Bill went rather glumly to the Forrest Primary School. Jim went with unknown anticipation to his first day in a job for which he had no training and no experience, but fortunately a very keen interest and enthusiasm, and Janet and I sat in the motel room and said: 'Now what?'

So to fill our time, we bought an instruction book, a couple of needles and some cotton thread and proceeded to teach ourselves to crochet. Big deal!

A few days later the four of us moved into our first Canberra home, an attractive rented house in the very pretty suburb of

Manuka, but there were no neighbours who welcomed us, no friends or acquaintances nearby, and certainly no children of Bill's age.

Jim's life became busier and busier, Bill continued, glumly, to go to school, Janet started her university studies again at ANU, and I found life incredibly dull. Fortunately, Peter and Doreen Butler and their four children lived in Canberra. We both knew them well, Jim through being related and I through my Mother's close friendship with them both. They were warm and welcoming, generous and hospitable and often very entertaining. We spent many good times with them. It was so good to laugh occasionally.

Jim's life became all absorbing. Mine was not. Jim travelled several times around Australia, made speeches, met many influential people, hosted several seminars at the new Institute and attended many dinners. Janet moved out to live with friends, cranked up her social life and occasionally had fiery arguments with her father about biological warfare and the value of Communism. Bill and I stayed home alone for many days at a time. Bill suffered extreme loneliness, far from the noisy, chaotic family life in Adelaide, and the warm companionship of the St Andrews school friends that he had known for six or seven happy years.

It was *not* a good time in my life and I was not particularly good at stirring myself up and making the best of it.

One day this poem tumbled out of me in a strange outpouring of loneliness and misery:

I dream of a man who is tender and warm,
Who holds me gently and keeps me calm.
He patiently listens to all my fears...
He quietly, softly dries my tears.

Then he speaks to me wisely and gives me hope
That today will be better, that I can really cope
With loneliness, sadness and distance from home,
That my useless existence can be overcome.

'He lets me speak of the sons that I miss,
Of my long empty days, of the gaping abyss
Where friends used to be, and outings and fun,
And my once busy life that is now totally gone.

'Again he listens, then speaks just for me,
Forgetting his problems and helping me see
That still I'm important, my value is high
And together we smile at this sadness passed by.

'I dream of this man ……. but I dream in vain.
God, give me the strength to survive …. and stay sane!'

MORE DISRUPTION

Then, early in 1974, Jim rang me from his office just as I was going out to visit Doreen Butler.

"Please can you put her off for a while,' he said rather earnestly, 'I have something to discuss urgently with you."

Oh, that sounded a bit alarming. My mind raced through all the awful possibilities that I could think of—all connected with accidents and serious illnesses. But when he came home his eyes were lit up with a curious gleam. "I've been asked by the Attorney General to go to Darwin," he said.

"But you've just come back from there," I answered with a sinking heart, thinking, *'another week of him away, another week of*

*Bill and me filling our dreary afternoons at the local Manuka delica-
tessen with our little treat of apple pie and cream'*.

"No, no. Lionel Murphy wants me to go to Darwin for good,
to become a Justice of the Supreme Court of the Northern
Territory… to work with Bill Forster, to help him in the Darwin
and Alice Springs Supreme Courts. There'd be quite a lot of work
with Aboriginal communities. After my time in Papua New
Guinea I have become very interested in the problems of traditional people and the White Man's Law."

"How long would it be for?" I asked in a small voice.

"Oh, it's a permanent appointment," Jim said cheerily, "and
such an honour. It's *really* exciting for both of us. The Government will provide us with a nice house, and a new car for me. And
you will even have a full-time house-keeper! We would probably
send Bill to boarding school, back in Adelaide at Saints, so you
wouldn't have too much work to do."

Exciting… NOT!! I was already bored with keeping house
for just three people after the never-ending busy-ness of cooking,
shopping, sewing and caring for six people in a rambling house
and a huge garden for the past 20 years. And if the neighbours and
locals were as unfriendly as I had found them to be in Canberra…
and why would they be any different?….. there would be very little
social activity to keep me from going crazy with boredom and
loneliness.

"But, but… I thought this move to Canberra was just for two
years and then we would all be back together in Adelaide again,"
I said, and by this time the tears were starting to seep through and
mess up my cheeks.

"Well darling, if you really don't want to go to Darwin we
won't do it. I can just go back to the District and Criminal Court
in Adelaide, back to my old job. It's not that bad after all."

Well… back in those days, in the early 1970's, no woman

in her right mind and with no particular earning skills of her own, would stand in the way of her husband's expanding career, particularly when it was a major promotion and would involve completely new areas of judicial and life experiences.

With a brave little smile, and a bit of a sniffle, I said:

"No… this is one decision that you will have to make on your own. I can't take that responsibility."

"Well," Jim said carefully, "I really like the idea of working in the Territory, of dealing with the unusual problems that arise in the Aboriginal communities. I like the idea of working with Bill Forster, we have been friends for many years now. The District Court in Adelaide deals with shop-lifting, loitering and petty theft. I could get extremely bored with that sort of work. I would like to accept this appointment. I hope you will come with me."

And of course I said "Yes," although my heart felt very heavy at the thought of endless empty, lonely days in another new environment, at the opposite end of the country from where many friends and my two older beloved sons were living and working. And *no way* would Bill be going to a boarding school if I had enough strength to oppose it.

That night we attended a reception for various Judges and senior politicians at Government House at Yarralumla. Not long into proceedings the Attorney General, Lionel Murphy, made a brief welcome speech and then, with a bit of a flourish, announced the appointment of…

'Mr Justice James Muirhead QC to the Supreme Court of the Northern Territory.'

It was a grand title and a grand moment, and I did feel a rush of pride that he was speaking of *my* husband. And I knew that I had a job to do, and a responsibility to fill as best I could in the role of background support to this man of mine who, here in the presence of many illustrious judges and politicians, in this beautiful old Government House in the capital city of Australia, had been so swiftly promoted to one of the highest positions that a lawyer can achieve. And he was not quite 49 years old.

Of course, everyone was very excited and full of congratulations and compliments for Jim's ability. And, of course, I felt very proud to be his wife. But *my* future still looked a little bleak.

A few days later I had a phone call from Janet. With her newly achieved Bachelor of Arts Degree she was working in a Darwin café and visiting her cousin Myranwy Kaines who was also working in Darwin, in a branch of Jim's old firm, Thomson and Co.

"Mum, Mum," she cried, having just heard the news of her father's appointment, "don't let Dad *do* this to you. You will hate it here in Darwin. It is so isolated. It is sooo hot. It is so messy. You will *hate* it. You just can't live here!"

(*Mmm…. Thanks Janet. Just what I need right now to make me feel good, especially with my increasing ability to feel sorry for myself.*) But I knew that she really meant to be helpful.

In the meantime, Jim had been invited to address a symposium at the United Nations and Far East Institute (UNAFEI)—a similar body to the Australian Institute of Criminology. UNAFEI was situated in Tokyo, and the Board of the Australian Institute of Criminology decided that this would be an ideal opportunity for Jim to visit several countries to the near north of Australia and spread the word of Australian research, and also to develop a good exchange of knowledge between the two Institutes.

This visit to Tokyo was to be followed by visits to Hong Kong, Malaysia, Singapore and Indonesia. The trip was to be for four weeks.

My heart sank again! Bill and I would rattle around by ourselves, without the occasional, but always stimulating presence of husband and father, for another lonely month.

But I, at least, had a lucky break. As the Institute was not well funded at that time, and it was not possible to send a staff person with Jim, (*'Thank goodness,' I thought, 'they are all much too pretty'*), it was agreed that I would go on the trip too and assist where I could, not only as bag-packer, but also in recording Jim's notes on a daily basis in preparation for the report that he was to provide on his return.

So, (*did my maternal conscience bother me at all?*), poor young Bill was now to spend a month without *both* parents, as well as his brothers, in this cold, unfriendly city, at a school that he was absolutely loathing. I consoled myself a little bit as Janet and her friend Jane Anderson, were moving into the house to be with Bill, to provide him with company, food and help with school. I am not at all sure that this arrangement was quite as successful as we presumed it would be. Canberra Grammar School, which Bill was now attending, was a fiercely traditional school, catering for the sons of diplomats and top public servants. The boys were addressed by their surname only. There was a disembodied voice, known as 'Sergeant' that disciplined the boys as they gathered in the quadrangle.

"Muirhead, take your hands out of your pockets… pull up your socks…" roared out over the air waves so that everyone could hear, and then sometimes point at the diminutive boy standing by himself in the concreted area amongst the very traditional arched stone buildings of this very 'establishment' school.

Bill hated it, and dreaded going to school, even throwing up in the toilet some mornings before Janet dragged him into the car to take him to this place of horror. Janet didn't like it much either, and, still carrying the extreme left-wing ideas that she picked up in Adelaide at the Flinders University, she happily gave Bill days off from school, convinced that there was absolutely no value in a posh, private-school establishment for her young brother's education.

In the meantime, the wonders and weirdness of our South East Asian travels were totally enthralling to me. Again, as in Papua New Guinea, and again much to my delight, Jim was focussing a little more on me. He depended on me to take down, in a huge notebook, his detailed report that he dictated to me every night after each action-packed day. Some evenings my pen just wobbled quietly off the page as I drifted off to sleep in mid-sentence. There was so much to learn and absorb…… perhaps that will be another story.

We were the only non-Asian participants attending the conference in Tokyo. We were very well cared for wherever we went. I met and spent time with women and men of the different Asian countries that we visited. I was included in visits to juvenile prisons where the emphasis was on education, occupation and training for a normal working life for the young men after they had served their term in prison. I listened to my husband give addresses that were translated into the language of that country. I ate strange foods at Japanese banquets, seated on the floor and entertained by geisha girls. I lived and cooked in a little Japanese house, making sure to take off my shoes at the door, and buying steak in 100 gram slices at the local market, and at great cost, with no common language to ease the problems of purchase. I sang 'Waltzing Matilda' with Jim, a little out of tune, at the cultural farewell at UNAFEI when everyone else performed exquisite and mysterious music and songs from their own countries, songs that dated well back into their ancient heritage. I waited apprehensively at the Jakarta Airport for Jim's late arrival in a separate car for our final departure. He had been taken on a rather secret mission by the personnel of the Indonesian Army to visit some Government unit that the Indonesian authorities seemed to think were important for Jim to know about. I never quite understood what it was all about, and I'm not sure that Jim did either, but I was very relieved when, in a convoy of Government cars he was at last delivered just in time for our flight back to Australia. And I *'shopped till I dropped'* in Hong Kong, buying a twelve person setting of a Royal Albert dinner set in preparation for the dinner parties that would be part of my wifely duties when we eventually settled in Darwin (*providing I survived the heat and horrors of that unseen and dreaded place*).

Then at last we were back to the realities of Canberra, and Jim wrote his lengthy report on his findings in the different countries that we had visited. He specifically mentioned the treatment and rehabilitation of young offenders:

"I believe we have much to learn from these countries in many spheres, particularly in the realms of public education, police and prison training methods and some approaches to the problems of delinquency." (1974)

He added to this statement in his Memoirs with the words,

"......when we look back at our own society today and the insecurity of so many citizens, both young and old, are we Australians really justified in preaching to other cultures about 'human rights'? I think not." (1996)

So now Darwin loomed darkly in the very near future. Jim had about six weeks to finalise his work at the Institute of Criminology, farewell his loyal and hard-working staff, his warm and hospitable cousins, the Butler family, clear his desk and set off to his next posting in The Northern Territory.

DARWIN 1974

On May1st 1974 Jim, Bill and I flew to Darwin for Jim to present his commission as a Supreme Court Judge of the Northern Territory. We stayed with the Senior Judge, Bill Forster and his wife Johanna, in their large old tropical house on the cliffs of Myilly Point. Included in their warm hospitality was a 'cocktail party' with crowds of totally unfamiliar but happily smiling faces which did nothing for me except to render me even more silent than I usually was at parties. I had already decided I was going to hate everything about this place and I was doing very little to change that resolve.

Just then I saw one face that I knew I had seen before. Tom Brown had been one of the few male dancers way back in my ballet days in Adelaide in the 1940's. He was in Darwin on a brief visit to advise on the development of the proposed Darwin Festival Centre. Tom and I disappeared into a corner and happily reminisced on our days in Joanne Priest's Studio Theatre and School of Ballet in which we had both featured for several years. So that wasn't too bad after all, but of course, he wasn't a Darwin person. He came from the 'civilised' south!

After a few days in the muggy heat of Darwin, young Bill and I flew back to Canberra to pack up our belongings that were still in the rented house that we had occupied during our fifteen months stay in this strange artificial city. We divided up all our bits and pieces for transport to Darwin and Adelaide, said goodbye, again, to the Butlers and to Janet, went back to Adelaide for more farewells to the boys and to Bill's friends, and then took the final journey to Darwin to start the rest of our lives in the Northern Territory.

Neither of us was too cheerful about this next upheaval.

On May 15th 1974 a rather solemn mother and son doggedly got on the plane in Adelaide, bound for Darwin with a stop-over in Alice Springs. Since his arrival in the Territory, Jim had been sitting on his first circuit in the Alice Springs Supreme Court, so he met us at the Alice Springs airport. He was surrounded by court staff; the Master of the Court, who was an Indian man, Jim's young female Associate, and several very pretty Court Reporters. Jim looked dazzlingly happy and very comfortable with all these new young people. I tried to look a little bit enthusiastic, but by now I had increased my self-imposed load of self-pity, and who knows what poor Bill was thinking as he headed for his third unknown school in less than two years.

After a 40 minute stop-over in the fairly run-down Alice Springs Airport building we all boarded the plane for Darwin. Jim, Bill and I were seated in the First Class section which should have felt luxurious and exciting, but didn't do much to lift my gloom. I'm not even sure that I even tried to put on a *brave little woman* act, even for the sake of appearances. Jim was very cheerful and chatty, smoking and drinking, both of which in those days were totally acceptable on planes, and he was obviously enjoying himself immensely.

After about an hour and a half of flying we bumped onto the tarmac at the Darwin Airport. We were met at the steps of the plane by the Chief Justice, Bill Forster and his wife, Johanna, and a few other vague faces, and loaded into a big black car and driven straight out of the airport. We were able to by-pass the tin shed that was the terminal of this isolated northern-most city of Australia. As the house that the Government had rented for us was not quite ready for occupation we were driven through the rather drab streets of Darwin to the Travelodge, the one and only high-rise building in town, all seven storeys of it! On the way there we passed funny little timber and asbestos houses set up on long thin iron legs, thick dry grass and straggly bushes. Old cars were the main things on display in most of the gardens. There was not much colour and no sign of people. Certainly not a bustling metropolis. What was this depressing out-post of a place that Jim had brought me to? The term, *for the rest of her natural life* was taking on a whole new meaning.

The Travelodge was okay. It was air-conditioned and had a large swimming pool and somehow our luggage had turned up safely in our room. Bill thought the pool was very grand and spent a lot of time in it, on his own of course. He also found entertainment running up and down the fourteen flights of steps that made up the fire escape well.

I should have been so very happy. The level of friendliness, welcome and hospitality was so warm and genuine compared to the icy Canberra scene. Jim Forwood, the uncle of Bill's school friend who had fallen into our pool back in those *lovely* Walkerville days, put on a cocktail party for us, making sure that there were people there who had moved to Darwin from Adelaide. The Travelodge had a grand party for the official opening of this newly completed hotel and included us as special guests. People made a fuss of us. They seemed happy to have us there, even though my conversation seemed to be limited to five or six words at any one time. But Jim made up for my shortcomings with his usual easy manner and cheerful chat.

And where was Bill at this 'grown-ups' party? Probably still running up and down the fire escape stairs... Poor lonely little guy.

After three or four days at the hotel we transferred to what was meant to be our temporary home where we would live until we found a house of our own choice which the government would then purchase for us. It must be admitted that Jim's terms of employment as a Supreme Court Judge of the Northern Territory were very generous: a house provided by the government at a minimal rental, a very nice car, all expenses paid, six weeks leave per year, first class air travel at all times for all three of us, *and* full time help in the house for me! And did even *that* make me happy? No... in the miserable state that I had got myself into?... of course not!

"But what will I do all day?" was my response to having the home help. "At least I'll do my own washing. I've got to do *something*," was my ungrateful wail.

"Yes of course, darling. I'll tell Nadine that you will do all our laundry," was my supremely patient husband's reply.

"Not the ironing though. It's much too hot to iron. She can do that."

"Yes of course, sweetie. I'm sure she will be happy to do the ironing. That will be fine. Nadine is French and seems very willing."

And so we settled into a two-storey, fully furnished, concrete block house, overlooking Kahlin Bay. It was late May. Darwin was just coming into the Dry Season and yet the heat and the unfamiliar level of humidity seemed to drain me of every ounce of the energy that I had always prided myself on. To walk up the steep concrete driveway, and then up the equally steep concrete stairs to get to the main part of the house turned my legs to two wobbly jelly-beans, and I needed to stop to regain my strength every three or four steps. Whenever possible I fell on the bed and slept away my misery.

Bill went off to his first day at Darwin High School. It was the beginning of the second term of First Year, (or year 8). Bill was extremely nervous and I was beside myself with fear that if he hated it as much as he had hated Canberra Grammar School Jim would insist on packing him off as a boarder, to St Peters

College in Adelaide where at least he would be close to his old school friends and, of course, his brothers.

What a long and anxious day that was. At 2:45 pm he was due home on the school bus. I held my breath and crossed my fingers. Then I heard footsteps pounding up the driveway, up the steep steps two at a time.....

"Mum, Mum," a hot and untidy boy burst into the house, "school was great. They called me Bill. They didn't call me Muirhead. The boys talked to me. Some of them asked me to play table tennis. Gosh—it was OK. Now I'm off to the Bay to go fishing. See ya."

And then began, in earnest, there in Darwin, what was to be, as we then thought, the rest of Jim's working life.

Jim was really happy. Bill was really, really happy. And I floundered miserably in my own particular puddle of self-appointed *un*happiness.

The Darwin that I saw in 1974 was made up of low grade, pre-fabricated houses, mostly on stilts. They were built on averaged sized blocks with very low cyclone fences and very, very untidy and unkempt gardens. The people I saw in the streets and in the shops were sloppily dressed, untidily groomed and spoke with drawling '*back-blocks*' accents. Even Bill remarked to me once as we drove past a couple of broad bottomed women meandering along Smith Street in bright red crimplene shorts:

"Mum, are you going to get fat like all those other women?"

That was *one* challenge that I was determined to accept.

In the City (*City?*) of Darwin there was one high-rise building which was the seven storey Travelodge where we had first stayed. It had lifts. The rest of the town was built on a grid of reasonably wide but dusty and dirty streets occupying a spit of land surrounded by the greeny-grey milky waters of the Arafura

Sea. There was one Woolworths store, a couple of Banks, a news agency, a couple of dress shops, various Chinese 'emporiums' and, surprisingly, *Alfred's*—the one shop that showed a bit of imagination in the wide range of goods and gifts displayed on its shelves. The rest of the town was made up of two storey government buildings looking boringly identical.

The social life of the place was slightly more interesting, although it still felt alien to me. Many of the people of Darwin had come there on a two year posting. For the husbands it was an uncertain step towards a promotion in their job back 'down south'. For the wives it was an opportunity to live a life of ease, even though it was a rather hot, sticky and challenging form of ease. But they all seemed to be enjoying their positions to the full, the men being big fish in a very small pond, and the women given opportunities to entertain passing dignitaries and enjoy positions that seemingly held a touch of prestige. Coffee mornings, Mahjong parties, sweltering, late afternoon games of tennis and golf, outdoor cocktail parties, dinners, suppers and occasionally the grand dress-up ball. It became a whirl of meeting, greeting and eating. And drinking, of course, drinking surprisingly huge amounts of alcohol.

Bank managers, heads of the armed services, insurance managers, heads of government departments, an occasional politician and *always* the Mayor and the two Supreme Court Judges and often the Administrator, equivalent to the Governor in the other States of Australia, were the main attendants at all the social functions. It seemed to be a constant round of social interactions. Were the people interesting to meet and be with? Not to me in my existing state of gloom. I only seemed to hear people speak of what they would do 'back home next year' when Alf or Rolf or Geoffrey got his expected promotion and may even finish up in *Canberra!! Joy!!* That they should be so lucky, to be on just a temporary posting to this godforsaken place.

On Day One of moving into our house in Temira Crescent one pleasant and surprising thing happened. There was a bank of colourful crotons separating our house from that of our neighbours. Suddenly there was a rustling of the dark red leaves, the branches parted and a bright smiling face poked through the bushes and a pleasant voice said,

"Hi, I'm Ruie Burkett. I live next door to you. The milkman comes every other day, the baker delivers every morning, the paper too, and there's a cup of coffee here any time you like," and she promptly disappeared.

So… this obviously wasn't Canberra. Was it possible that there might be a show of friendliness somewhere? But I still had a long way to go to shake off my black gown of self-imposed misery.

One bright spot in my life was the fact that Reta and Brian Caddy and their three children—long term friends from South Australia—had come to live in Darwin a couple of years before we arrived. They were lovely, easy-going, fun-loving people who appeared to thoroughly enjoy all the personalities and differences that Darwin had to offer. Later I learned that Reta had sat in abject misery, covered by sand fly bights, make-up dripping off her face, in a sub-standard house for the first few months of their arrival, and it wasn't until she found employment in air-conditioning at Paul's Milk Supplies that she came to a happier approach and acceptance of all that Darwin had to offer.

The Caddys were people we could totally relax with, and they laughed a lot. And the quiet, gentle 'Uncle Cad' became a valuable and much loved person in young Bill's life.

Jim was always cheerful at this time and came home every day for lunch to help break up my long, empty days. He was enjoying his work, his colleagues, and the informality of his professional and social life.

A brilliant move on his part was to take Bill and me on a

day trip to the Adelaide River, about 60 kilometres south east of Darwin, where we joined Stefan's Safari Tours. The good looking European Stefan took us on a small motor launch, and then on an even smaller aluminium dinghy up the waters of the Adelaide River and into the wetlands of its tributaries, where, he said, we would see crocodiles.

We chugged slowly up the wide river, which to me felt and looked like the '*great, grey-green, greasy Limpopo*' River of Rudyard Kipling's 'Just-So' stories. The muddy banks and long grass, straggly trees and occasional wild bird provided a new and interesting landscape. Not a sign of human habitation was anywhere to be seen, and when the motor was deadened the quiet of the moist tropical air settled warmly and peacefully all around us. We lunched on a delicious macaroni salad, provided by Stefan's wife, and then we all transferred into a tiny dinghy which Stefan propelled through the narrow waterways that crisscrossed the grassy wetlands. He was determined to find a crocodile, but nothing had surfaced so far.

Suddenly Stefan stood up in the back of the dinghy, pointing ahead, and revved up the engine. We hung on nervously and saw in front of us a small mob of big black wild pigs, desperately swimming across the shallow creek, frantically trying to escape our noisy intrusion.

Stefan pulled out a small revolver from somewhere. Two ear-cracking shots rang out and the pigs moved even faster away from us, leaving one of their group floundering helplessly about 50 metres away in the swamp. With no hesitation Stefan leapt out of the rocky little boat, splashed through the shallow murky water, put one more bullet through the unfortunate pig and whipping out a bush knife from his belt slashed through the two hind legs of the animal and proudly carried them back to present one to us as a trophy of the day's outing.

Probably fortunately, we still hadn't seen any sign of a crocodile.

By this time the sun was low in the western sky and as we re-boarded the larger boat and moved gently back down the river to our land base the sky started to take on the most beautiful orange, pink and rich red colours, birds came to rest in the trees, sounds of frogs and insects filled the air, and a wonderful peace settled on this empty and strange landscape. And some of it started to seep into my unhappy soul and stealthily began to work its magic. This was an unspoiled and mysterious place and I was being given a rare opportunity to be touched by it, to be embraced by it and to absorb it if only I was willing. I could feel some of my tightly locked edges gradually opening up to drink a little of it in. It was a very important moment of hesitant understanding.

Happily for Stefan as we neared the landing jetty one large crocodile was basking in the rosy light of the early evening on the muddy bank across the river from us. Hearing our engine, this huge, knobbly creature slid quietly into the still water of the river and without a sound it gradually sank out of sight. We had seen a crocodile. Stefan had fulfilled his promise.

ALICE

Our next trip out of Darwin was to Alice Springs.

Jim was due to sit in the Court down there, and as it was school holidays he decided to drive down to Alice, a distance of about 1,500 kilometres, taking Bill and me with him. Tim and his lovely young girlfriend, Michele, were up on holidays too, so we made up a pleasant car-load. It was a good journey through empty and ever changing scenes. We stopped often to explore huge rock formations, or leafy water holes, the temperature gradually dropping as we moved south.

We filled in the driving time studying Peter Slater's bird book, trying to identify all the different birds we saw on the way. Bill and I occasionally tried practising the Bahasa Indonesian that he was learning at school and altogether we were quite a jolly car-full.

Alice Springs was a small dusty town with very large, beautiful white gums growing in a wide, dry, sandy river, the Todd River. Our accommodation was a weird little lean-to that had been tacked on to the old Court House in the centre of town. A small kitchen, a miniature two-bedroom sleep-out with a tin roof and a minute bathroom set in the angle between the two sections became our home for the next two weeks. Walking through the sleep-out led directly into the Judge's Chambers, still small but with an open fireplace, and then directly into the Court Room. A patchy lawn outside the kitchen with a big apricot tree growing beside it formed our unfenced outside area. The car was parked on the edge of the lawn, and the Jury Room, a small asbestos box, just big enough for twelve people, was just beyond the car.

It was Okay. It was quite good. It was *cool* and it was not *muggy* and humid. All at once my legs started working properly, the feeling of malaise and exhaustion that dogged my every movement in Darwin was completely gone. I almost sprang as I walked. I felt a normal 47 year old again. I probably smiled a little more often.

So this change got me thinking.

Darwin was where I would be for the rest of my life. So far Darwin had made me feel old enough to just lie down and sleep for the rest of those years. This wasn't a good way to spend the rest of my life, however brief a time that may be. If I could feel okay in clear, crisp weather I had better make up my mind that I was going to be okay in hot muggy weather, or there was no future for me at all.

SO GET YOUR ACT TOGETHER, MARGARET!!!

Ten days later, driving back to Darwin, we passed through Katherine and the tree-covered hills that start to develop between Katherine and the little settlement of Adelaide River. Gradually the air became hotter and moister and, surprisingly to me, that warm clammy cloud that started to settle around us seemed to fold itself more gently around me, welcoming me back and inviting me to accept its friendly warm embrace. It was telling me that there was a good home for me in this strange remote town of Darwin if I would do *my* share of helping to create it.

So back in Darwin I got busy finding something to do to fill my days. A new friend suggested that I could become a courier to accompany heavily handicapped children as they were driven to and from school, and Red Cross welcomed me as a Meals on Wheels helper delivering hot meals to a number of the aged people in their homes. Both of these 'jobs' gave me opportunities to meet the *real* people of Darwin, the people who lived there permanently, and not always in very comfortable circumstances. Strangely, the energy that I had found in Alice Springs stayed with me. I could *almost* run up those steep concrete steps at the front of our house in Temira Crescent and I started playing tennis in the late afternoon on Audrey Kennon's black surfaced tennis court, staying on for drinks afterwards, dripping happily into our after-tennis beers and being devoured by sand flies.

Parties became fun. New faces became interesting. People were friendly, warm, generous. Darwin was GREAT.

During our stay in Alice Springs Jim had made sure that I saw as much of the surrounding country as he had time for. We went to all the nearby gorges, taking picnics *and* bottles of fly spray. Sometimes there were patches of water holes that we could cool our feet in, and spectacular gum trees grew lusciously and

determinedly in the dry river beds. The colours and formations
of the rocks were spectacular, and ferns and small trees grew out
of cracks in the rocks, and at Stanley Chasm small rock wallabies
hopped in and out of the ledges of the steep escarpment that
hung over a shadowed water hole.

I could not help but be impressed by such natural beauty and
grandeur.

And there was one outstanding trip that we did during these two
weeks in Alice Springs.

Geoff Eames, the lawyer for the local Aboriginal Legal Aid,
and later to become a Judge in the Supreme Court of Victoria,
was determined to get the 'new Judge' to meet the local people in
their own environment; to hear *their* views of the 'White man's
Law,' and to hopefully develop a better understanding of the many
problems faced by the outlying Aboriginal communities and the
rebellious and culture-damaging behaviour of their young people.

So we set off in the government-provided car to drive to the
remote community of Papunya, a settlement in the desert area
about 240 kilometres north-west of Alice Springs. Geoff drove in
another car, with a few passengers, but he had a couple of special
people for us to take in our car.

An Aboriginal man from the Papunya community had just
been released from prison and his brother had come into town
to accompany him back to Papunya. They needed a lift so Geoff
seemed to think it would be a good idea if they travelled with us.

And of course it was. This was my first close encounter with
members of the Aboriginal people. And in the confined area of
the car it took me back to those enlightening days in the Courts
of Papua New Guinea. There was definitely a similarity in the
atmosphere surrounding our two special passengers.

One of the passengers was very chatty, and although I didn't understand too much of what he was saying, when we passed through a certain rocky dry creek bed, he became extremely excited, pointing out to us that this was where his brother had tipped the village truck over, hurting one of the many passengers in it, and completely ruining the truck...... the *only* one available at that time at Papunya. The other man sat silently and stolidly ignoring all his brother's excitement.

What we didn't know until quite a bit later was that, as soon as the two men were delivered back to the community, the man who had been in prison was to be surrounded by the elders of the community and was to suffer the tribal punishment due to him for the crime against his people that he had committed. Consequently, when he alighted from the car, this poor fellow who had been almost trance-like during our journey, walked down to the edge of the village, sat with crossed legs and awaited the spearing of both legs, which was the prescribed punishment.

Unfortunately for him, the police of the village decided that it was not appropriate for all this to happen while The Judge was in town, and so the poor guy was put in the local lock-up, a tiny tin shed, until Monday by which time The Judge would have safely left and they could get on with life in their own way.

In the meantime, George, a middle-aged elder, was instructed to take us all for a drive to get us away from the scene that was meant to take place, though we knew nothing of the reason for this. He showed us the school and the bare red dust oval where the bare-footed kids were happily kicking footballs around, and then drove on outside the town towards magnificent and distant red and purple hills. In total ignorance I asked him if they had cattle in those hills and if the children could play there.. He rolled his beautiful liquid black eyes at me and said, "Nooo, no cattle. There's snake."

"Many snakes there?" I asked.

"NO! No. Only one snake. One big, big snake. He eat the cattle, he eat the children, he eat me if I go there."

Oh. I stopped my dumb questions and let Jim do the talking.

The rest of the weekend was uneventful for me. But we were taken to the fairly new art centre. In 1973 a resident artist had come to the town to interest the young people, especially the boys, in painting on canvas with acrylic paints. As the older men of the community watched this happening they said,

"We could do this. We tell our stories in the sand, but we could make them better by telling them in paint."

And so they had started painting. The canvasses were simple and unframed. We bought some as they were very cheap. We were interested in the stories they told, and one in particular, in purples and reds. The old man who painted it was not well at the time, but he was asked to come from his tent to talk to the 'big law man.' The old man, Tim Leura, came and told us his story, but for his own and, I guess traditional reasons, he told me one story and told Jim a completely different one. He also said that we must keep the painting folded as we carried it away so that the women could not see what it was.

"Men's business," he said firmly.

We slept reasonably well on the floor of the Nurse's house and left late the next day. But during the visit Jim had been taken by the elders of the community to sit down and talk about the White Man's Law. He was shown the traditional punishments that were used in the community, and he was taken to some of the sacred sites where special tokens and important implements of initiation ceremonies were concealed amongst the rocks. He was sworn to secrecy, which, of course he honoured for the rest of his life. The only comment he made was, 'I do those Aboriginal kids a favour when I put them in the Alice Springs jail.' But of course he had also learnt that traditional punishment was still very much in use. And as George had said on the diversionary drive he took us for, 'I had the punishment once.' (another roll of those luminous eyes), 'I never do wrong again!'

I AM WOMAN...

Back in Darwin, Bill was very happy at Darwin High School, fishing and throw-netting every afternoon. Jim was *very* happy in his work. And I was actually starting to enjoy this life that I had been thrown into—both the social life and also my little bit of voluntary community involvement. Richard and Janet were both travelling overseas. Tim seemed happy enough at University and was still with Michele. So, apart from missing them all desperately, why should I complain?

Then later in the year, about September, I was at a women's luncheon in someone's home and Rose Gurupatham, the Executive Director of the YWCA of Darwin, was chatting to me over our glasses of fruit-cup. She was a very small, beautifully sari-clad Indian woman, and she said to me,

"Margaret, next year, 1975, will be International Women's Year. A declaration from the United Nations states that it will be celebrated by women all around the World, in every Member Nation. It is an important call to women all over the World to stand up and have their say, to be heard and to be listened to. The Australian Government is supporting it, and the Prime Minister, Gough Whitlam, has even appointed a woman to be his advisor on women's affairs. But we must do something for ourselves here in Darwin. We will have a public meeting at the YWCA and invite the women of Darwin to come together and make plans for 1975. We must show the community what women can do, how they *can* develop their innate skills and demonstrate their full potential as valuable members of the work force and the important contribution that they make in the home in creating the generations of our future. It is up to us to show the true strength of the women of today."

"Oh," said I—the very average housewife, the totally unambitious, dependant wife, the mediocre mother—showing a polite but very mild interest in what Rose was saying.

"Yes," continued Rose, "and, Margaret, I think it would be excellent if you would chair that meeting."

Goodness me! I had never chaired a meeting in my life. I had only ever attended one or two meetings for school mothers where I had said not one word, but had watched in admiration as some young mother very capably got us all organised for the next school fete. Me?? Chair a meeting?? A meeting where I didn't even know the women who would be there?

But somehow I could not find a viable reason to say "No," and to my amazement, and horror, I heard myself saying, "Well, Rose, I suppose I could do that." *Gulp!*

The date for the meeting was set; Wednesday 23rd October 1974. The meeting would be held on the large veranda of the YWCA Hostel in Smith Street. Rose, having no idea how terrified I was, promised to send me information on the purpose and the aims of this special year that was to be dedicated to the needs and achievements of women of many different cultures and nations through the world.

I was cornered!!

But instead of ringing Rose the next day and stammering that I couldn't possibly do this thing, for a myriad pathetic reasons, I was invited by Lucille Arthur—a long term Darwin resident, Armenian by birth, lively, attractive, confident—to attend a full-day seminar run by the Women's Electoral Lobby (WEL). And again, to my surprise, I accepted. (*Who did I think I was?*)

But this meeting was an amazing experience for me. It was led by Sarah Douse, the assistant women's adviser to Gough Whitlam, the Prime Minister of Australia. Sarah was quietly spoken, a tiny bit nervous, but full of information and enthusiasm for what women, especially young women, could do to improve their image in the community, to increase the awareness of women in all walks of life and to reach up and out to fulfil their own dreams of achieving a stronger position in their families, their communities and in the work place.

Then the young women, mostly young mothers, took their turns on the podium. I was amazed; they were so eloquent, confident, strong but not strident. They spoke of the need in the Darwin community for a play group, childcare, nursing mothers' group, community education, more attention to women's health, part time work, equal pay and the need for a women's refuge. They also spoke keenly of the need for some form of financial recognition of a woman's work in the home.

Overall, the strongest message that I heard was not: 'So the Government must do this and that for *us*. They *owe* us!' but: '*Each* of us can form a small group and we will work together to create these valuable services which are, so far, non-existent in the suburbs of Darwin. And together we will present our case to the Government, both Territory and Federal.'

It was extremely educational for me, and certainly quite in-spirational food for thought, to prepare me for this forthcoming meeting.

And so the dreaded day arrived. Rose had sent out an impres-sive letter to:

'*All the Presidents and Secretaries of Women's Groups in Darwin,*' outlining the aims of the United Nations' declaration that 1975 would be noted as International Women's year. '*Equality,*

Development and Peace,' were its aims and, *'…Mrs J H Muirhead will chair the Meeting'.*

Sixty women came to that meeting!!

Rose introduced me as the Chairwoman(!!), probably emphasising that I was the *wife of Mr Justice Muirhead*. There was no other attribute or accolade that she could pin on to me… housewife of 25 years?… very reluctant camp-follower?… average sort of cook?… deserting mother?

So, I took a very deep breath, somehow calmed my shaking hands, and launched into my laboriously written explanation of what International Women's Year was all about for us women of the Territory, outlining the benefits of making the dream of "Equality, Development and Peace" for all women the aims and results of our efforts.

And I finished with what I hoped just might sound like a rousing call to the women sitting around me:

"…that throughout 1975, the International Year for Women, we will work towards increasing the status, dignity and responsibilities of women."

There was polite applause, and then, the first question:

"Why!"

"Umm, why what?" from the still shaking Chairwoman.

The young tie-dye clad, earnest, bare-foot woman sitting on the floor just in front of me, nursing a small child, replied:

"*Why* do we need the United Nations to tell us women what to do? We all know about our freedoms, and about our rights, and we know we're as good as men, better actually."

I wish I could remember my response, but to my never-ending amazement I managed to come up with something that widened the scope of the Year to include women of all ages and abilities, and seemed to interest the other 59 women on the veranda, even if the challenging and vocal '*hippie*' at my feet didn't look too impressed.

Anyway, something must have worked okay. Maybe some of the skills of the young women of the WEL Bird's Eye View Seminar had seeped into my brain. Whatever, the women, with great enthusiasm and a bit of skilful leadership by Rose Gurupatham, decided that a committee should be formed here and now and that, obviously, I should be the Chair of that committee!

OH MY HAT! I hadn't counted on that horror. But how could I say 'No' without looking, and feeling a total fraud and proving to everyone (including myself) that I really *was* completely inadequate for any sort of public activity.

There was eager acceptance of nominations to the committee by 7 or 8 women, including, to my inner but I hope well concealed concern, the young woman on the floor with her child. Every one of those women, was fully or part-time employed at some useful and valuable level in the community. There was a teacher, an accountant, a social worker, doctor, business woman, secretary and an Aboriginal worker.

Oh my! What was ahead of me I wondered.

And I wondered this even more at our first meeting. All these clever women were seated around our dining room table at 21 Temira Crescent in Larrakeyah, waiting for me to get things moving.

I pinched my leg a few times, *was this really me?* And, after the polite and easy part of '*thank you for coming*' etc. I asked for suggestions on how we could fulfil expectations and hopes for the coming year of 1975.

And the suggestions came thick and fast.

"We need a child care centre. Somewhere we can leave our

little kids while we have some time off. Darwin doesn't have any
Grannies or Aunties to help us with babysitting. There aren't even
any play-groups in Darwin."

"Oh yes, I see. Um…. How do you suggest….?"

"Easy. I have a couple of friends who see the need as much as
I do. We'll put together a plan."

"Oh. Okay…… er…. Good."

"We should have a stage play, about women, acted by women,
written by women, staged and managed by women. Show the
boys what we can do."

"Oh yes, ….um… what do you suggest….."

"Oh, there are women at Brown's Mart, (the one theatre
in town) who are itching to do something like this. We'll put
together a plan and bring it to the next meeting."

"Oh, that's nice."

"A women's health centre. Male doctors know nothing about
women's health issues – periods, menopause, pregnancy, even
the bothersome irritation of thrush. '*Just a natural part of being a
woman*,' they say."

"A competition in schools for an essay about the role of
women in our community….. to raise awareness in young
people……..make them question a bit before they fall into the
stereotype of thinking that we were all brought up with…….I'm
just a housewife, my husband does all the important things, sort
of attitude."

"An open forum on why women are not in every section of the
work force, including top management, and why they don't get
the same pay as men do. How about a woman Prime Minister."
And this brought roars of self-mocking laughter.

As if!

And so the afternoon went on. I was overwhelmed, and
secretly in panic mode, at the huge tide of plans, the actions and

the enthusiasm that were rapidly mounting around my ordinary, homely, dining-room table. What had I found myself embroiled in? I had *no idea* how any of these ideas could come to fruition. I had absolutely no experience of any of these areas of work that had been covered in the past two hours. I would have no idea of where to start with any of them.

But, somehow, I made notes as the women were speaking, and finally drew the meeting to a close with a summary of the projects that had been agreed to, and the person who was to work on that project. I made a date for another meeting, farewelled them all with smiles and thanks, and sank exhausted on to the couch.

Exhausted, yes, but strangely elated and a little bit excited. I had survived this incredible, action-packed meeting. I had somehow dug up the ability to manage a group of energetic and independent-minded women who were creating a raft of positive projects aimed at changing how the world we lived in looked at the role of women in our community. I had not stammered or stumbled and revealed my very real lack of experience and confidence in myself. I was still '*just a house-wife*', but maybe... maybe... just *maybe* I did have something more inside me that wanted to come out and be more visible outside of my accepted role of wife and mother.

And somehow, after this long, and most certainly enlightening and energy-filled meeting, although each woman had gone away with what seemed to me to be a really daunting task, I had, thankfully, finished up with no specific job to do except wait, still very nervously, for the next gathering when we would hear if any of these dreams had really started to take shape.

We only had time for one more meeting before Christmas of 1974. This was a time when all public servants, and many other workers in the top half of the Northern Territory, had six weeks annual leave. Because the Christmas was the rainy, stormy time of the year, many families 'went South' to escape the humidity, heat and sandflies, and to spend time with the families that they had left in other parts of Australia. The women of the newly formed International Women's Year NT Committee were no exception, so this second meeting was relatively brief but, oh so positive. Every one of those women had made a start on her project and had gathered around her a group of equally enthusiastic young women who were all ready and fired up to get moving with their plans for the new year. So 1975 was going to be a great year, with big changes coming in the status of women.

"We'll show'em," they muttered.

Rose Gurupatham was delighted. It really was her baby after all. I was simply doing her bidding, but she did seem to be quite pleased with me too.

Ardotte at home in Glenelg. 1928

Ardotte, a bit chilly in the Grampians, with
Bruce, Mum, Keith and Helen. 1932

At Kangaroo Island, taken by Dad. 1938

Adolescence. 1942

Ballet days, as Harlequin, with Lynette Tuck. 1940

Dad and Mum. 1942

Engagement Day! December 11th, 1948

Chair of IWY. (With Jan Landsdowne, Secretary.) 1975

Wedding Day! February 4, 1950. St Andrew's Church

The Family at Walkerville. 1968

Christmas in Darwin, 1978

Dawn's Silver Pendant

Government House, 1989

Investiture in the Order of Australia. 1988

And then...

The whole family in Tuscany, 2011

The Grandkids in Tuscany.
From top left - Kit, Katie, Hannah, Jamie, Julia, Tim, Jesse, Chris, Joshua. 2011

Janet, Richard, Tim, Bill at Donnelly River.

Still having fun. 2016

Off to the Cabaret in Adelaide. 2016

SECTION 5
FINDING MARGARET

MISSING TRACY

In early December of our first year in Darwin, 1974, Jim had his final sitting for that year in Alice Springs. I waited for Bill's school term, Year 8, to end before we both joined Jim in the little lean-to flat at the Supreme Court of Alice Springs. As we were leaving Darwin there were warnings of an approaching cyclone. We didn't think too much about it, though Jim's Associate, Peter Summerton, was a bit restless about leaving his family in Darwin in case the cyclone blew up into something serious. But cyclones had skirted around Darwin every Wet Season, so we were told, and they never caused much bother. And so it was with this one.

"Just another fizzer," people said.

And, "Only piss and wind," Jim stated happily, as he always did.

After a few days in Alice Springs, enjoying the dryer cooler weather of the Red Centre, Bill and I left Jim to his Court work and to the local end-of-year celebrations with his Court Staff, and went to join Tim at 'The Acorn' in Adelaide.

'The Acorn' was a four-roomed bluestone cottage in St Peters that we had bought with the leftover money from the very quick, pre-Canberra sale of our much loved family home in Brunswick Street Walkerville.

It was Tim's second home since we had left Walkerville. The first had been a small, run-down cottage in Unley (with the rather grandiose name of 'Tytherington'). This is where we had left him in Richard's care and taken Bill with us to go and live in Canberra in January 1973.

Surprisingly, both the older boys had managed extremely well, in spite of heavy frowns from the Pulteney Grammar School mothers. Richard finalised his Town Planning Degree, and Tim, through sheer doggedness and determination on his part, passed his final year with good enough results to be accepted at the Adelaide University to study for an Arts Degree.

I had not been at all happy at having to leave two of our sons without a parent's control and support. Jim didn't seem to mind at all, and I later learned that the two boys thought it was absolutely great. I am sure that Tim grew up a lot faster during that time than he ever would have if he had still been living at home with his parents. One unpleasant lesson he had learned was being given a Saturday detention for taking time off during recess to collect his dry-cleaning that no-one else was able, or willing, to do for him. He also received an occasional caning for not wearing his cap. This was probably compensated for by the other things that he learned in a house full of noisy and adventurous young university students, doing all the wild and woolly things that university students have done since time immemorial. With a mother's concern I wrote a very serious letter to Richard, stating that I was not happy that Janet Lockie, the lass in Richard's life at that time, was sharing his bedroom, and of course, his bed. I received an equally serious letter back from Richard telling me that as Tim would understand the nature of the true love that existed between him and Janet, it was really giving Tim a good example of adult life. Hmmmm.

Fortunately it was much later that I knew of other activities that Tim was learning about, including the inhalation of things that I hardly knew existed!! But—he has assured me many years later—learning through observation *only* at this stage of his life. It seems that, through a conversation with a Canberra cousin, he had sworn off alcohol and drugs, and stuck to that till he got to London many years later, where he finally tried the inhaling 'stuff'.

So they survived, and Richard and Janet Lockie set off for overseas travel at the end of 1973. Tim remained at 'Tytherington' (which really was a very grand name for a very ordinary dwelling) with a couple of Richard's friends, and, after working through his holidays delivering furniture, proceeded with his University degree.

Later in the next year, after we had settled in Darwin, 'Tytherington' was demolished, (thankfully not by the boys and their mates), and so we decided that Tim and a couple of his friends would move into our little 'retirement' cottage in St Peters. Because there was a small oak tree growing near the front gate, Tim promptly christened the house, 'The Acorn'.

And so it was to 'The Acorn' not too far from our dear old house in Brunswick Street, that Bill and I came later in December 1974 to prepare for our first Christmas back in Adelaide.

It was heaven to be back in a cooler climate again and to spend time with old friends and young relatives, and Bill was delighted to have at least one older brother around the place. Jim arrived from Alice Springs just a couple of days before Christmas Day, and we decided to go to the local Church on Christmas Eve for the Carol Service at midnight. We took communion together and there was a great feeling of warmth and friendship about us. And yet, I was strangely overcome at that moment by a profound feeling of sadness and loss. Was I really missing Darwin after all? Here I was in Adelaide, my home town, where I always wanted to be, and yet uneasiness and melancholy were clouding my joy. And tomorrow was Christmas Day to be spent with much of our family.

With no small children to get us started early in the morning, we all slept in a bit on Christmas Morning. Idly I turned on the radio to hear more Carols, but...

'... and it seems that the City of Darwin has been completely destroyed by a most violent cyclone. Little news is coming through yet as all communications seem to have failed.'

This was not possible. This is just a stupid story. Not on Christmas Day. What could be *really* happening.

I rushed into the others, who were gradually waking up, and quickly told them what I had heard.

Jim grabbed the telephone and rang numbers that he knew in Darwin. The phones rang but there were no answers. We knew that the Forwoods, the Arthurs, the Kennons and the Caddys were all staying in Darwin for Christmas. They couldn't all be out and not answering their phones.

Gradually snippets of information filtered through from odd phone lines in Darwin that miraculously still had a connection.

It was, unbelievably, absolutely true. Darwin had been hit by an enormous cyclone. Winds of over 200 kmh had completely destroyed all the outer suburbs, and most of the rest of Darwin. Cyclone Tracy had slipped around the Tiwi Islands and headed straight for the City. Having done her first devastating damage, the eye had passed over the city, giving relief and hope to the people who were sheltering wherever they could. But then the other side of the Cyclone hit—winds travelling in the opposite direction, more powerful and vicious than before—and Cyclone Tracy completed her destruction of the few buildings, trees and gardens that had been left unharmed before.

We had no idea what was left, who was alive, or what would happen to people who were still there. And we had no way of finding out. Darwin had gone. This place that had welcomed us so generously seemed to have been blown out of existence.

No school? No Courts? No house? No job?

It was a very sombre Christmas Day as we waited to hear more news.

So much has been written about The Cyclone. Countless stories, tragic, miraculous and occasionally wryly amusing, have been told.

We were not there. I do not have a story...

Except perhaps, this: this is where the second part of my life starts to unfold.

AFTER TRACY

On 30th December 1974 Jim was able to get back to find out what was really left of Darwin. A friend with connections in the Air Force was able to squeeze him on to a Hercules aircraft, where he was jammed in amongst a huge cargo of generators that were being sent to Darwin to create some power for the stricken city. He had a little more space to move after Alice Springs because, when the Hercules landed there for refuelling, it landed with such a thud due to its overload of generators, causing considerable concern to the pilots, that several of these great bulky things were dumped in The Alice to avoid any problems landing in the turbulent air of the Top End. Fortunately Jim was not included in the off-load as, at that time, his weight was just under eighty kilograms.

Jim's arrival in Darwin brought him total shock at the extreme devastation of this northern-most city of Australia. He headed straight for the Courts to find out all that he could of the fate of his profession and the Court staff, and to consider the distant possibility that there might be any sort of future for anyone in that area, other than for scrap collectors and rubble removers.

"G'day mate, have a warmie." He was greeted by his old friend Brian Caddy.

"You can doss in with me in my office in the MLC building if you've got nowhere to stay. No lights, no power, but plenty of warmies," said Cad, smiling as ever, as he pulled the top off another luke-warm Fosters ale.

On New Year's Eve Jim rang me from the MLC building on one of the few phones that was still connected to the outside world:

"Well darling," said a surprisingly cheerful voice, "it is all quite unbelievably terrible, *but*... the Court House is still standing though it has been badly battered and my car has been stolen by some kids who came up from Lameroo Beach, and who have now headed south in it. *And* they have taken my Papua New Guinea bow and arrows and other special things from my days in the Court there as well. Our concrete block of a house has a few broken windows and a leaky roof but it is still standing. The Government is opening a school for any kids that are still here and the few lawyers who I have seen so far are keen to get active again. If I can get a permit for you and Bill, you can come back at the beginning of February, but only if you really want to. There won't be too much social life. It won't be too much fun. You will need to find something useful to do. Maybe a job...?"

Another dramatic change of lifestyle coming my way? But my heart soared. Darwin and all that it held had become so very precious to me. Of course I wanted to go back.

The next day Bill drooped in from Victor Harbour where he had been staying with Matthew Portus, a school friend from his early years at St. Andrews and St Peters College back in the Adelaide days.

"Matthew's parents say that the Government won't bother to rebuild Darwin. It's not worth it and there's not much use for it anyway, mostly filled with Public Servants."

"Well they're wrong," said I gleefully. "Dad rang and said we can go back if we want to."

Bill straightened up, standing three inches taller. The colour came back into his cheeks and his large brown eyes lit up.

"Great!" he said, dropped his bags on the floor and went into his room.

Jim arrived back at The Acorn a few days later. He had the precious piece of pink paper that stated that we could return to Darwin providing that we had somewhere to live, some money and a job.

So, on 1st February 1975 we all flew back into Darwin. Jim immediately drove us around the Northern Suburbs. The absolute silence was totally eerie. No trees, no people, very few vertical power poles, not even any fences. There were just rows and rows of bare stilts on which the prefabricated houses of Wulagi, Milner, Anula had once stood.

Our very solid house at 21 Temira Crescent, protected by the cliffs and an overhanging cyclone fence of the Larrakeya Army Barracks, was, miraculously, still standing. Our landlord, Mr Gerucci, had spent all of January replacing iron sheets on the damaged roof, and panes of glass in the shattered windows. He and his wife had taken up residence in our downstairs games room, and two other couples, who had survived the Cyclone but had lost everything that they owned, soon moved in to our two spare bedrooms upstairs.

And so another new phase of our life began.

Brian and Reta Caddy and Laurie and Wendy Kirkman, our new housemates, were all back working at their old jobs. They were all still fairly traumatised by their terrifying experiences of December 24th. They were coping amazingly well, but at dinner each night there was only *one* subject for conversation, *The Cyclone*, occasionally interrupted by a loud and rasping '*Oggie*' from Wendy to their floppy-eared, slobbery-mouthed Basset Hound as he slurped up the last of our dog, Spot's, dinner.

Of course they needed to talk and talk, and of course we needed to listen and listen, well aware of a certain sort of guilt that we felt as we hadn't actually *been there*. But occasionally after dinner Jim and I would slip out for a beach walk, just for a little space from all those appalling stories, the losses, the tears, and even the brave humour. But, as Jim had said, I needed to *do* something with my days, (other than cook dinner for seven every night).

So what on earth could I do??? I couldn't even type.

Then I thought of Rose Gurupatham of the YWCA who had somehow wangled me into that bothersome involvement with International Women's Year all those long months ago, and which I quietly hoped had been blown away with the Cyclone.

So I called in to the 'Y' to see if there was anything useful that I could do there.

"Why yes Margaret, of course," said Rose. "Now, could you run a women's group for me. There are so many women now living in really difficult conditions. They need the support of other women who are living in happier conditions, and I'm sure that you are one of those women."

"Oh no Rose. I wouldn't be any good at that sort of thing."

"Ah. How about leading a Keep Fit class. These women need healthy diversions too."

"Oh, I don't have any qualifications like that, Rose."

"Maybe activity groups for children. They have so little left in their lives now."

Another shake of my head.

"Well, Margaret," said this slightly exasperated small Indian woman. "I have no staff left at all, and I have this big hostel to run. All 72 beds are occupied by the relief workers who have come to Darwin to start the clean-up. I can find a cook, Mrs Meaney is just wonderful. I can probably find house-maids. But I can't run the office *and* keep the cash books in order. Will you *please* do the books for me?"

"Oh Rose, I'm just a house-wife. I have no training for *anything*. I can't even keep my cheque book straight. I would be useless at keeping your books and all that banking and stuff."

Poor Rose sounded exasperated.

"Margaret!" she pleaded, "will you please *try!!*"

How could I say 'No' to that desperate plea; to this small, dignified person who had sheltered 'her girls' through the trauma of Cyclone Tracy, herding them into the concrete corridors of the three storey building which was the Hostel of the Darwin YWCA to protect them from whatever damage the Cyclone might do to this reasonably solid structure? She had had to endure so much, and was still prepared to keep the Hostel going to house a gang of working *men*. The YWCA, the Young *Women's* Christian Association, had hardly *ever* allowed a male person past the front door. But on December 24th 1974 many things in Darwin changed forever.

So, on the following Monday morning I arrived, nervously, at the barred window of the very small front office of the YWCA of Darwin in Smith Street. Elise Carter, a young woman from the National Office of the YWCA, had come from Melbourne to give Rose support and assistance in managing the Hostel, now mostly filled with construction and rescue workers, and a handful of permanent women residents. The building was still leaking slightly from a damaged roof and a few windows that still needed to be repaired. Elise took me on as her willing, but woefully inexperienced, new assistant.

She took me through the Kalamazoo system of receipting all payments. She showed me how to manage the telephone system, to keep the Gestetner (a sort of copying machine) properly inked and oiled, and how to carefully count, package and record all the cash for banking. I worked from 9.00 am to noon each day, brain spinning with facts and figures, and constant interruptions at the barred window of the little office from residents and visitors. Then I limped home to some sort of lunch for me and Jim before collapsing exhausted onto the couch for an hour's recovery sleep, after which I greeted Bill home from school at 2.30pm.

Mind you, Bill didn't need much attention. He would almost immediately race off to his afternoon fishing spree in Cullen Bay, which was still a small shallow inlet of sea just below our house. With the huge tides in Darwin it would alternately be completely void of any water when the tide receded, or lapping around the mangroves that grew around its perimeter. Bill had a throw-net that his beloved 'Uncle Cad' had given him and had also taught him how to handle. This kept Bill happy for most of the afternoon, until the huge red sun sizzled into the warm Arafura Sea.

Bill would watch in fascination when an Aboriginal woman —a regular at Cullen Bay—threw her handline into the shallow waters, pulled out a large, wriggling fish, threw the line in again bringing in another fat shiny fish, and picking up her freshly caught dinner, wander off home. Bill would throw and throw and throw and, at best, collect a couple of tiddlers, and the odd small crab. But it was enough to keep him happily addicted to the mysteries of those shallow waters.

INTERNATIONAL WOMEN'S YEAR

So now I was a 'Working Wife', even if only part-time, and at the end of each week I took home a small yellow envelope with just a few dollars in it. But they were *all my own*!

I found the work at the 'Y' very satisfying. I had always enjoyed counting money and adding up columns of figures. In the first few years of our marriage, way back in 1950, I kept a small note book, recording in it every penny that I spent, then adding it up and subtracting it from the £3.00 housekeeping that I received from Jim, and banking the amount I had saved. And I still have that little note-book. Maybe I was a frustrated manager way back then?

At the time that we were married, in 1950, Jims's pay at the

Law firm of Thompson, Ross & Lewis where he was employed was Five Pounds Ten Shillings per week. The basic wage was Five Pounds Seventeen and Sixpence per week. We paid my mother thirty shillings per week for our rent, so that left Jim One Pound for his own spending money. It was a tight budget.

But now, in the front office of the YWCA, I had a small adding machine that printed out all the figures for me. I just had to make all the numbers from the Kalamazoo sheet, the Petty Cash book, and the banking records match up and agree with each other. Typing was not on my agenda. Rose had to do that for herself. But talking to the strange array of people who came to the office window came surprisingly easily to me, and handling the phone calls was a breeze. I was actually having *fun*, and working at a *serious* job!

Unfortunately the 'fun' part was soon marred a little by the fact that Rose, with her energetic enthusiasm for the betterment of the status of all women, brought up the matter of International Women's year again. I was so sure, and indeed had hoped, that this had all been blown away forever, at least from The Territory.

But now Rose had me On Site, and securely under her small brown thumb. And as she reminded me, I *was* still the *elected Chairwoman* of the IWY Committee for the Northern Territory.

So she rallied the remnants of the Committee, added a couple of extras, and there we all were again, discussing all the plans for The Year. *Oh dear!*

Perhaps I felt a smidge more confident as we gathered for our first Post-Tracy meeting. I was now a Working Woman after all. From my limited observations in working at the YWCA I was able to see other women in the work force. I saw women being capable and productive, and not just occupied by the hum-drum activities of washing-up and changing nappies and hostessing afternoon tea parties.

Much to my surprise all the previous plans for IWY were still firmly in place, and somehow Rose had organised a pile of T-shirts with the IWY Logo printed on them. We all started to wear these with pride, and sold them to anyone willing to accept the words, 'Equality, Development and Peace,' that were blazoned on them.

Rose had also made sure that a photographic exhibition, put together by the National YWCA for IWY, would come to Darwin, and that I was the person who would open that exhibition. And that meant I had to make another speech!! But strangely, once I had put my facts and figures together I found that I could almost chat informally and eagerly to the fairly large crowd of women who had come to share this unusual exhibition and, hopefully, to buy the book in which the photographs had been recorded. In making that speech, I was largely inspired by the fascinating and frank black and white images of women in every stage of their lives. These included—somewhat alarmingly for some of the more conservative people—photos of women in a same-sex relationship, and also a woman openly breast-feeding her baby. (This was after all, still only 1975)

So something must have been happening to my minimal sense of self-esteem and ability since I had come back to Darwin. My son Tim, who was born with invisible extra-sensory antennae glued to his head, certainly noticed something about me had changed. Later he told me that, after his first University holiday in Darwin during that unusual post-Cyclone year, he went back to his friends in Adelaide and said: "I've got a new Mum. You wouldn't recognise her. She talks a lot more, seems to have her own opinions on all sorts of things and even seems to know what is going on in the rest of the world. And what's more, Dad seems to quite like the new her."

Another plan for IWY was that, as a celebration of the survival of Cyclone Tracy and the re-emergence of the women of Darwin and their families, we would hold a Gala Dinner on the MV 'Patris'. This was a large Greek passenger ship that had been brought into Darwin and tied up at the Darwin Harbour wharf. It provided accommodation for the 400 or so public servants who had come back into the stricken city to get the wheels of bureaucracy running again. This dinner was to be managed entirely by women, and men could come if they were willing to. We decided to use the occasion to honour Dr Ella Stack, the first woman in Australia to be elected as a City Mayor. We also invited Mrs Margaret Whitlam, wife of the Prime Minister, to be our guest speaker. Everyone co-operated wonderfully. The chefs of the Patris, supported by the management, arranged an excellent menu for the occasion. The main dining room of the big ship was booked out by the women of Darwin, and many of their husbands and partners who seemed to be quite willing to accompany them to enjoy one of the very few festive functions to be held at that time in the ragged social life of the recovering Darwin.

There was a minor but scary skirmish with the Social Manager of the 'Patris' who rang me just a couple of days before the day of the Dinner, protesting that we had not invited any of the resident passengers to the dinner. He stated that they were totally offended by this omission and so they had planned a boycott of the Dinner and were going to refuse to let any of us, *including the wife of the Prime Minister*, come on board. Oh my hat!

After a 45 minute phone call between this man and me, he and I eventually came to an uncertain but mutually agreed settlement, which mainly involved inviting some of the women residents who were housed on this great ship. But my brain was working overtime during those long minutes… Where do you put a large and important woman like the Prime Minister's wife when she arrives to attend a dinner that has just been cancelled by a Residents' Social Committee? And where in the ruins of Darwin could we find a sheltered space large enough for a dinner for 350 people?

But somehow I had won the argument with the young protester and the Dinner went ahead as planned and, as I wrote in my report to the National Committee for International Women's year:

> *'The Gala Dinner… was attended enthusiastically by women, and reluctantly by men who later expressed enthusiasm and praise for the organisation of the evening and for the six speakers, all of whom were women, and all of whom wisely and to their credit, kept their speeches brief.'*

A dinner may seem a frivolous way of acknowledging the serious business of women 'making their voices heard in the community'. But for the women of Darwin who were managing their families' lives in very, very basic accommodation, living under the elevated floor boards of their previous homes, with walls consisting of canvas and fibre glass sheeting, and taking showers under the fire hydrant (if it was still working) in their street, a formal night like this provided them with a very welcome evening of sanity and normality.

Another seemingly frivolous achievement of our IWY Committee was to persuade women's groups Down South to send us cosmetics and undies for the Darwin women whose personal and important precious bits had been blown away. None of these could yet be bought from the very few re-opened shops in the town.

And the IWY Committee was achieving much more in the interests of the well-being and advancement of women in the

Territory. We managed to extract, from Canberra, the $1000 that had been given to all the States of the country. The ACT had received that amount of money from the Government with the idea that *if* the Northern Territory '*did anything*' they could share the money! As we knew we had plenty we wanted to do, and urged on by Rose, I made several phone calls to Canberra. Amazingly, I managed to convince someone that, although the community of Darwin was still in tatters, we women were very busy with our plans for IWY and we deserved the right to have our very own funding. So with this money to boost our energies, we were able to finance many projects. We provided airfares for women in outlying areas to attend a women's seminar in Darwin; we helped the Nursing Mothers to get re-established; we set up a small play-group/child-care centre; conducted an essay competition—'The Cage Door is Open, but the Canary Won't Fly'—in the few schools that had opened. We funded the production of a play, 'Sweetie Pie,' for and by women, and we started the establishment of a Women's Crisis Centre. $1000 surely went a long way back in 1975.

It was a magic year, and did so much for the morale of the young mums and the women who were stoically re-establishing their shattered lives and families in this remote northern city of Australia.

For many people in Australia, including a majority of women, the fact that the United Nations General Assembly declared that 1975 would be celebrated as the International Year for Women passed completely unnoticed. Women continued to fulfil the roles of wife, mother, cook, cleaner, nurse, gardener, wailing wall, and sex partner for their men throughout the country. The woman was the silent, unrecognised partner in a man's life and well-being, although she had the major responsibility of bringing his children safely through their childhood and developing years.

Certainly, in return, she usually had a home to live in, clothes and food included, but her voice was very small when it came to most decision-making, and her only income was the house-keeping allowance doled out to her by the bread-winner.

For me, having been brought up with the same attitudes as these women, IWY threw open a door that I hadn't realised existed, and this door opened onto a big wide world of possibilities that I had never imagined could exist for me. And this growing world was made even wider by my increasing involvement in the developing activities of the YWCA of Darwin.

IN CHARGE AT THE 'Y'

So, in amongst all this giddy activity, the Hostel life at the YWCA became busier and busier, and Rose had started to include me, as an observer, at the monthly Board Meetings of the 'Y'. Of course, it helped no end that I was the *wife* of Mr Justice Muirhead, and Rose, in her strategic Indian way, made every such post a winning post, making sure whenever she applied to the Government for help that *Mrs James Muirhead* was very much a part of the 'Y' scene. And I did find it all wonderfully stimulating and didn't mind at all what extra hours I put into both the YWCA and IWY. I was learning *so much* all the time. Added to all of that was the fact that Jim seemed to be totally approving of all that I was doing, and he didn't seem to resent the extra times that I was not at home.

Bill was extremely happy to be safely back at Darwin High School and, with his very close school friend, Andrew Cole, scavenged the beaches for scraps of metal and bits of houses that had been buried in the sand by the ferocious onslaught of Cyclone Tracy. But he also, no doubt, felt sadly neglected at other times by his parents who were so wrapped in their own activities. Luckily, though, the house was still well occupied by the Caddy's and the Kirkmans *and* their dog, so he was not often left alone.

And of course, to make it all so much easier for me I still had Nadine coming in every morning to clean and make beds and restore the house to a high level of cleanliness. But at the end of each demanding and always stimulating day I was unbelievably exhausted.

And then I had dinner for seven to prepare.

So, rather bravely I thought, one night after our fellow house mates had eaten the dinner that I had cooked, I suddenly said,

"Right, whose turn is it to cook tomorrow night?"

"Ooh" said Reta, "yes well...I guess it could be my turn."

How easy that was, after all.

After I had served just a few months as part-time bookkeeper/ office girl, Rose announced that she was moving on to another area of work that was more to her liking. Working for a hostel filled largely with *men* had never been on her agenda, and she had found herself another job, a more suitable niche developing programs with Aboriginal women, within the Uniting Church.

Surprisingly, Rose asked me if I would take the position of full-time Executive Director of the YWCA of Darwin, "... even just for 6 months. *Please*, Margaret. You have developed such a good understanding of the work and ideals of the YWCA. You seem to have a good working relationship with the Board and the Staff. I think you can do the job and do it well."

With a bit of further encouragement from the President, and an assurance that they would be able to find a '*properly trained YWCA person*' for the job within the next few months, I nervously said that I would give it a go, "but only for six months at the most!" and that I would just "do my best". I really had become so involved in the daily dramas, the interesting people who passed through *our* hostel, the little successes and the occasional words of praise that came my way. I knew that I would miss it terribly if I went back to just being a home body again, with coffee mornings and an occasional game of tennis or Bridge to fill my days. Rather to my surprise my part-time job of book-keeper/office girl, interspersed with the developments of the International Women's Day Committee which had exploded into many community activities, had opened up my world to experiences I had never imagined. My real education in life was just beginning. My learning curve was straightening up to be a steep 'J'. And, even more surprising, I found that I could give a good impression of knowing what I was doing, and even occasionally making an independent and successful decision to help '*get things done*'. I was feeling good about all that.

So, on the first Monday of September 1975 I arrived at work – (*me, the little housewife, going to work? Full-time? Goodness me!*). I stopped in the front office to chat to Mary, my lovely young co-worker, and now my *secretary*! I think she had a fair idea how nervous I was feeling. We had often joked: 'what on earth does Rose do in her office all day? Make phone calls and read magazines?' And now I was going to sit in her place and find it all out for myself.

Eventually I said,

"Oh well, I'd better go up to Rose's... er, I suppose '*my*' office."

And reluctantly and ever so slowly I mounted the ten steps up to Rose's recently vacated very tiny, eight foot by eight foot, glass-doored office. And there I was; the brand new, totally untrained, inexperienced, and overwhelmed Executive Director of the YWCA of Darwin.

Now what to do?

I didn't have to wonder for too long before the phone calls started coming in:

The Insurance assessor......

"When can I talk to you about the claims for the damages to your building by Cyclone Tracy? I found Rose impossible to deal with—she expected everything to be done *yesterday*. I hope you won't be so difficult." (*As if I knew anything about insurance! Jim had always handled all that sort of thing.*)

The Manager of the YMCA......

"Can I come and talk to you about the re-development of our community programs? Nothing has happened since the Cyclone."

The cook called from the kitchen......

"I need a new kitchen hand. Nancy tells me she is pregnant and can't stand the smell of stew and can't keep working here. "

The Secretary from the Department of Community Development........

"We can probably help you with that grant that Rose was looking for, to help subsidise people who seriously need accommodation but can't afford to pay much. There are so many people living in ruined corners of broken houses. You are the only organisation that can provide shelter."

The President, Gwen Stolz...

"Well, Margaret, I hope you are settling in okay. We really should have a Board Meeting *very soon* so we can get our women's programs going again. Also after-school activities are so badly needed for the children."

And so my days were filled... Filled? They were bursting... And so was I. I felt that I was running in six directions at once. At the end of each day had I really achieved anything, except a completely muddled head?

So I contacted Richard. I remembered the days, way back in Adelaide, when he was studying for his Town Planning Degree, and used me as his guinea pig in a time and movement project that he had to produce. As I was cooking dinner he sat and mapped my every movement, sink to stove, stove to cupboard, cupboard to bench, bench to telephone.. etc etc. The resulting plan looked very much as my head felt. I certainly failed the efficiency test.

In response to my plea for help, Richard suggested that I should keep a daily record of everything that I did, every phone call, interview, letter, staff encounter and tea break. And he also sent me a book by Peter Drucker about management. I read it avidly. I think the best lesson that I picked up was to 'pass the responsibility *down*.' It did seem to work quite well. As 'the boss' you can't possibly know everything or do everything yourself when there is a staff of 20 women, and with a Board of another 20 women, each of whom had their own particular area of expertise, or at least some knowledge or skill. By giving other people re-sponsibility for their part of the whole job you can form a team of people who each has a sense of 'ownership' and hopefully an increased interest in the success of the organisation.

Richard also advised, "Make sure your office door is always open!"

The other very useful advice that I received was from Jim. "When possible, sit down with all your staff for a morning tea break. It's a good time to share gripes, plans and potential problems."

And also, from Jim, "Remember, you have to *spend* money to make money."

So, following Jim's first advice, almost every morning of the week, at 10.30, the hostel supervisor, secretary, book-keeper, community worker, youth worker and I all left our desks, sat down in the middle-floor lounge room of the Hostel and shared chats

and cups of tea. The house and kitchen staff did the same on the
balcony outside the large dining room of the hostel, overlooking
a huge banyan tree and a fern-filled creek. It was so productive
and helpful. Petty jealousies and misunderstandings were aired
and usually settled. Plans and ideas were often developed. People
learned about each other's area of work, and sometimes their
families. I learned so much from all of them. There was a pretty
good feeling all round.

And so I set about surviving my allotted six months.
Sometimes in the middle of the night, thinking how to settle an
ongoing power struggle between two of the staff, or planning the
next fund raiser, I would actually count, *to the exact minute*, how
much longer before my six months was up and I could be finished
with this enormous job and no longer have to worry about the
myriad problems, questions, decisions, demands that were constantly bombarding me.

And yet… and yet… towards the end of February 1976,
nearing the end of our agreement, when Gwen Stolz asked me
if I would consider staying on as the Executive Director for a bit
longer, my answer was a resounding, "Yes please!"

So, what was I learning in that steep J-curve from the 'Y'? I
learned to connect with, and appreciate the real skills of women.
I learned to watch, and to listen, to absorb and to learn. I learned
to enjoy women from different life styles, different nationalities,
different religions. I learned from a poster that I had seen in the
Darwin Cathedral, showing two black feet beside two white feet
with the caption,

'*I like you – you're different.*'

The Adelaide measuring stick of acceptability—'*how you hold
your knife,*' '*how you pronounce the word dance*', '*what school you went
to*', '*no dear,* you *must not go out with a Catholic boy*'—evaporated

completely. I learned to accept, I learned to listen, I learned to make decisions and I learned to hug.

For five and a half long years I was Executive Director of the Darwin YWCA. I went to National meetings in Melbourne with women from all the other YWCA's in Australia. I met skilled and dedicated and *inclusive* women from every part of the country. From them I learned about meeting procedure, running workshops, role play groups, speaking out, being heard, accepting people as they were, not as *I* thought they should be. And I learned to cope with Government bureaucracy and even politicians. And family life and official functions with Jim still went on around me, and they seemed to fit themselves in amongst all this fascinating and rewarding busy-ness that had taken over my life.

GRANDMOTHER: SURPRISE!!

Towards the end of 1975 we had a full gathering of the whole family in Darwin. This was very exciting for me as I had lived for these past three years without, at any time, all four kids being together with us at the same time. Janet, having just returned to Adelaide from an extended working holiday in Europe, had flown up to Darwin with Tim who had just completed the second year of his Bachelor of Arts at the University of Adelaide. Richard with Janet Lockie, his girlfriend of some years, flew in from Kuala Lumpur where Janet's parents were living. Richard had ridden a large motorbike across Europe and Asia with a long-suffering, but adoring Janet Lockie on the back, having many interesting adventures on the way. They had been away for 18 months too, so it was going to be a wonderful reunion for all of us.

What a joy it was to have them all together again. So much to talk about, so much to share. Such excitement all round. We had a grand celebratory dinner. For me all the most precious pieces of my life were all there, around the rosewood dinner table. All so happy.

In a moment of quiet, somewhere between the roast beef and the pavlova, Janet said quite perkily,

"Guess what? I'm pregnant."

"OOoooaaahhhh".....The air rushed out of everyone's highly inflated balloons.

"Oh dear," said Jim, surprisingly quietly.

With a bit more vehemence, and thinking of the varying array of men that Janet had dated in Europe and elsewhere, I said,

"And just *who* is the father?"

Janet looked at me in shock,

"Why, Tim Ewens, of course." (Tim had been the first love of her life.)

"Oh, so he is coming home?"

"Oh, no. He doesn't really want to be involved. I can take care of it all by myself."

I was stunned. Janet was in tears. The boys looked blank.

Janet Lockie took a deep breath and said:

"It's not going to be a puppy, Janet. Having a baby is hard work."

Then *she* burst into tears.

And Jim said very quietly, and with a tiny smile:

"I'm going to be a grandfather" and gave Janet a gentle hug.

Gradually we all calmed down, and settled in for the night. I was flooded with so many mixed thoughts. For some weird reason, babies had never been very high on my ladder of emotional needs. But if there *had* to be one to my single daughter, thank goodness we weren't still living in Adelaide where the Walkerville *Old School* set still sat very solidly in judgement of anything outside the accepted conventions. I cringed inwardly at the thought of coping with their looks and expressions. But added to that were a jumble of different values that I had learned and experienced during the past super intense developmental year at the YWCA, *and* International Women's Year. I had come to recognise, so late in life that, most certainly women had rights, far beyond my own aspirations, but with those rights, and of equal importance, there were also serious responsibilities. And to me, to have a child without *two* parents to develop its life and well-being was decidedly and seriously irresponsible.

But Janet was my daughter. She had made her decision. She, and our friendship, and our family as a whole, were very precious to me. And Jim, as always in a family crisis, was surprisingly calm about it all.

And so it all came to be. Janet stayed with us in Darwin and worked at the Library for a few months and then went back to Adelaide to await the birth of her baby. It was due late in May 1976. She asked me if I would come down to be with her at the birth. To my continuing shame I told her I was unable to. I wonder, now, what stopped me? I know that I worried enormously as to my ability to go through the very painful and traumatic experience of witnessing the birth of a human baby, especially my own daughter suffering that struggle. I still was pretty rigid about showing any emotions. And I was also, selfishly, completely absorbed in my work, and imagined that I couldn't leave it for the uncertain period of time that a baby takes before deciding to join this mortal world.

Jim, on the other hand, with his in-born and unswerving belief in the power and value of '*the family*', took time off from his much more demanding and important work and flew down to Adelaide to be with his daughter. Unfortunately, the delivery date was later than expected and he had to return to Darwin before he could meet his first grandchild, but I am sure that his support and presence was of enormous value to Janet.

And so, as she has done all her life, Janet, with her amazing resilience and independence, '*did it her way*', and a healthy, perfectly finished-off baby boy was born.

And *then*, at last, something went '*ping*' for me and I hopped on the next plane and flew to Adelaide to meet my very first grandchild, Joshua James Muirhead, born on 22nd May 1976. And I *melted*. To hold this warm little body, to see my daughter's face in his tiny little features, to know that he was also a part of me, awoke in me such a flood of warmth and love that has never wavered, equalling only the rush of love that I felt when Janet was first placed, warm and sticky, on my shoulder, twenty-five years and forty-nine days before.

Jim was ecstatic. He created a huge banner and hung it over the balcony at 21 Temira Crescent in Darwin:

'I AM A GRANDFATHER'

He had just turned 51 and was so proud. His sense of family and the continuity of life had been fulfilled.

'Who cares if there is no father," was his attitude, "Janet has a strong family to support her and her son. I will always be there for my grandson."

And so he was in so many, many ways.

WOMEN OF THE WORLD

Probably my greatest thrill of working with the YWCA was being elected to go to two International Conferences where women from 83 different countries met together to discuss the problems and limitations that had been traditionally imposed on so many women, particularly in the developing countries. These conferences were held in 1978 and 1979, in Fiji and in Athens. They also aimed, and were wonderfully successful, at strengthening understanding and forming bonds between women of many different cultures. And I was there in my own right! I had been specifically selected to represent my country! I was not just a tag-along wife with no role to play. I had a vote, and a voice.

And on one disconcerting morning, at the beginning of a fully attended plenary session, that voice was suddenly called on by the Chairperson of that session. She called to me,

"Margaret. The girl who was to open this session with the morning Devotional has pulled out with nerves. We have to get started somehow. Quickly. Sing something!"

And Nita Barrow from the Caribbean, the wonderful National President of the World YWCA, prodded me towards the podium.

So there, in front of 300 women, in their different coloured skins and beautiful national costumes, in a large lecture theatre at the Athens School of Theology, I took a deep breath, maybe even whispered a tiny prayer, opened my mouth and sang the Conference anthem:

'A new commandment I give unto you
That you love one another as I have loved you...'

And it happened! My voice came out full and clear, and gradually all the women joined me, in whatever language was natural to them, voices from all over the world, swelling up through that lecture theatre, joining together in perfect unison. It was a pure moment of peace, harmony and love. And I was surrounded by it and held firmly in its midst.

Another memorable time was dancing on a beach on a warm, tropical evening, with women from Africa, Fiji, Samoa, Greece, Papua New Guinea... all in the colourful dress of their country, dancing together, singing and embracing, seemingly fulfilling the motto of the Conference..........*'Like a Child'*.

It was an evening full of joy.

Much later that night, in my dormitory bed, I scribbled down how the evening had affected me.

'Like a child – I did not want to leave....
The evening was too fresh, too gay.
We joined together, and we danced and sang.
The sand was in our feet
The sea was in our hair
And love was in our hearts.
Women together – joined in love and joy,
Black and white – yellow and brown,
Divided by language,
But united by love.'

Almost forty years later, my beloved sixteen year old grand-daughter, Kit, repeated this poem in her own words and from her own perception, having heard the story from her ageing grand-mother some few years earlier. I was heartened, and honoured, that *she* had listened.

'Like the reflection of sky on sea
Veins of oak mirror creased hands
And stained lips caress the warmth of tea
As her eyes recall the lands.

I sit quiet, not requesting to disturb
And as she sips the dust soaked air
She invites me to her world.

Beneath the velvet sky she danced
With salt between her pores
Along the coast of Pacific earth
With tunes that traced the shore.

She speaks of different coloured skin
And hair of different shades
Although as one they sang and cheered
Below the same sun's rays.

The moon would show its bulbous cheeks
Whilst the tide would stroke the sands
And still the women danced on forward
With my grandma, binding hands.

She called it serendipity,
The moments that she trusts,
  And presently I sit amidst a city
  Of memories and resting dust.'

In Athens I listened to the women of Africa saying:

"You know, when the fighting stops, we won't have anything to talk about,"

And:

"I was so annoyed with my daughter. There was shooting in our street, and Miranda just stayed at her desk doing her homework and she should have been under the bed as I've always told her."

In Fiji, Hilda Lini, a beautiful young woman from Vanuatu, then known as the New Hebrides, bowed her head and wept as she told us of the struggle of her people to gain their independence from the French *and* the British who shared the colonising of the New Hebrides. She told us, "… when the British Queen was visiting the Island the authorities demanded that the young men should demonstrate their custom of displaying their bravery to their community by jumping from a very high platform with just a plaited vine tied around their ankle. But," she said angrily, "this was the wrong season when the vines are dry and brittle, and the first young man to take the leap crashed to his death as the vine snapped as it tried to take his weight. And this had been ordered simply to entertain a woman from the other side of the world," Hilda finished up bitterly.

This was in 1978. Just two years later, in 1980, Hilda's brother, Father Walter Lini, an Anglican priest who had led the struggle for Independence, became the first Prime Minister of the newly independent Vanuatu. I am sure that Hilda would have become an active and vocal member of the new regime.

I had many beautiful and mind-changing experiences at these two international conferences. In Fiji, we slept in sixty bed dormitories at a girls' school, The Adi Cakobau (pronounced *Andi Thackambow*) School, in the hills outside the colourful Capital City of Suva. The showers were in stalls separated by low partitions of plywood. The soap was placed between every second stall. One morning as I reached for the soap a finely boned, delicate and very dark-skinned hand reached for the soap at the same time as I did, and was followed by a gentle giggle,

"Ooooh, look at that," said a young voice – then a black foot came up beneath the dividing partition, and I put my much paler foot beside it. Another gentle giggle and:

"Aren't we different."

When we emerged from our showers there was a very beautiful, and very dark skinned Hetty, from the Solomon Islands and we smiled and hugged.

In Athens we did a *'getting to know you'* workshop where we sat on the floor with a woman from a different country. We followed the directions of the leader in learning a little about each other, listening and repeating what we were discovering. At the end of the session we were told to demonstrate in words or actions how we felt about our 'partner' and what we had learned. The young woman with me was from Samoa. Samaria was very young, very shy, and English was difficult for her. How was I to explain to her what I had learned from her, the privilege I felt at being trusted by her as she shyly and hesitantly spoke of her family and village life. I didn't need to think at all. I put out my arms and wrapped them around this beautiful young dusky skinned girl in the warmest, most sincere embrace that I had ever used for another woman. She responded with tears in her eyes,

"Ah, now I have a *real* friend from Australia."

And for me, who had always shied away from showing outward emotional affection, it was like a tightly closed magnolia blossom, learning to open its great white perfumed petals to let the warmth of human love come in and make it grow.

I could go on and on… and on, about the many warm experiences that penetrated deep into my heart through those two YWCA conferences. I think of them as 'Margaret's Magic Moments', and they changed my thoughts, attitudes and, I hope, actions towards my fellow beings for the rest of my life

WOMEN AT THE 'Y'

Back in Darwin, in the Post Cyclone days at the YWCA, every day seemed to bring a new surprise, a new challenge, and, from time to time, a new crisis.

Because there was no low cost or even crisis accommodation for the many displaced people in Darwin, the Northern Territory Government gave the 'Y' a Grant to subsidise the boarding costs for people who had no place to live. Our three storey hostel building was the only place of its kind left standing after the furious onslaught of Cyclone Tracy. So our 72 beds were always fully occupied. Although traditionally, for years, the YWCA had been strictly for women only, the Cyclone changed that completely and forever. We were open to everyone. And what a strange cross-section of the drifting community came through our doors.

A young man who insisted on taking the sheets from his bed when he was leaving the Hostel because '...*they are Jesus's raiments and I must look after them for Him*'.

Another slightly older man who had been living in the one remaining corner of a totally damaged house by the sea in Cullen Bay moved into one of our dormitories with the Government grant subsidising his board and lodging costs. He often came to my office to talk about the problems that he had faced in the last few years. But after a couple of weeks he decided that I was not cared for properly by my husband and, on pink note paper, he wrote graphic letters to me of how *he* would give me *exactly* what I needed to make sure that I became '*totally satisfied*!!'

So many misfits and disturbed people came to us for shelter. A woman, discharged from Ward I, the Psychiatric ward of the Darwin Hospital, was very restless and unhappy until she 'took over' an Aboriginal woman who was staying on the same floor as her. Marina, the Aboriginal woman, was strong, proud and totally blind. She filled her time knitting brightly coloured squares for rugs... "*I love these bright colours, don't you?*" she would say. But Esther, from Ward I, insisted on guiding Marina down the stairs, cutting up her food, and even trying to feed her! Eventually Marina—who was perfectly independent and capable—had to beg us to keep Esther away from her.

Annie, a pregnant 16 year old girl, whose parents couldn't cope with her predicament and her behaviour, and Alice, a 17 year old deaf mute roomed together because Annie, who had a heart of gold and had endeared herself to all the staff, thought that she could help Alice to cope with her loneliness and rejection by her family. It worked wonders for Alice until one day Annie came home to find Alice rummaging through Annie's few belongings and claiming them as her own.

All hell broke loose. There was a screaming chase all through the Hostel until Alice disappeared. No one could find her. I had a thought. I went into the toilet block on the top floor. Just one booth was occupied. I climbed up on to the seat of the adjacent toilet, and there was Alice, head down, clutching Annie's precious bits and pieces. Of course she couldn't hear me puffing and panting as I reached up and leant over the top of the dividing partition and grabbed her by the back of her collar. She let out an almighty yelp of terror, and then sullenly followed me to my office. It was the end of a promising friendship. Annie eventually had her baby, but when I asked her if it was pretty she said,

"I couldn't look. It 'urt too much, and I'm not allowed to keep it anyway."

We were sad to see her leave us, but some months later she married a man with three children and she would often come back to visit us and to borrow a vacuum cleaner or a floor polisher, and she told us that she was happy. So she was safe in her marriage, but obviously hadn't selected a millionaire.

Miriam, an Aboriginal woman, married to a non-Aboriginal man, drank herself silly every day when her husband was at work. Our Hostel Supervisor, Mrs Denton, a dour but soft-hearted Scottish woman, worried about Miriam, and one day asked her if she was able to sew or knit or crochet or make *anything*. Shyly, Miriam said she could make baskets and mats but she didn't have any leaves or roots to work with. So Mrs Denton popped her in the staff car and off they went to the bush for the day, coming back with arms full of prickly pandanus leaves, and roots of several different plants. Miriam settled herself under the huge banyan tree at the back of the Hostel, stripped the leaves into thin strands with her thumb nail, built a small fire and boiled a billy, soaking the leaves and the different roots in the water, creating different colours for dyeing, and proceeded to weave the most beautiful, intricate and colourful baskets and mats, with not a drop of alcohol anywhere in sight. Her works of art were proudly displayed in the front office and Miriam was a new woman, flashing her brilliant white smile as she collected the dollars that we were able to collect from selling her skilfully made artefacts. Her husband looked so much happier too. One of those mats still graces my kitchen shelf.

Our first Vietnamese refugee family was a stunning, and sobering, experience for us all. When the American forces eventually pulled out of Vietnam, in 1973, after years of abortive and disastrous fighting in that controversial war trying to hold back the Communist forces from the North, thousands of South Vietnamese families were left homeless and hiding, in fear of their lives, from the overall confusion that the Americans had left behind after their misguided invasion. This invasion had come as a result of President Nixon stating, in 1954:

"...... *to avoid further Communist expansion in Asia and Indochina....... we must put our boys in.*"

60,000 of those '*boys*', as well as many Australian 18 year olds, unfairly conscripted by ballot, were killed, and many more wounded and mentally traumatised before America at last recognised the futility of this '*un-winnable war*' and withdrew her troops.

They left behind, of course, tragic chaos in this bombed and scavenged war-torn country.

Families who were able to, paid much gold to the owners
of small boats to gain a very risky way to escape the inevitable
hardships and possible death that would be inflicted on them if
they stayed in their native land. Australia, as she had done in 1975
when she took in 2,500 East Timorese who were fleeing their
war-torn country, was again willing to take in these desperate
South Vietnamese people, asking Australian communities to
provide shelter for them and where possible to provide work for
the man of the family. A call for help went out to all community
organisations and churches, as well as to private individuals, to
offer this support.

At the YWCA we knew that we could help. One of our larger
bedrooms, which had its own bathroom, was ideal for a small
family, and we had been told that 'Vietnamese people are very small',
and one of our quieter Board Members, Beatrice Watkins, said
that her husband could give the Vietnamese father a job at the one
and only milk factory in Darwin where Graham was the manager.

We were all very excited at this new, and for us in the 1970's,
unusual experience of being involved with refugees. All the arrangements were made, and late one evening Beatrice set out for
the airport with a Vietnamese woman, My van Tran, who would
be her interpreter. The plane was coming from Singapore, and
many tourists and travellers poured out of it. But there was no
sign of a small Vietnamese family. Beatrice was terribly disappointed. She and My van Tran were about to turn away when a
young pilot came up to them and said to My van Tran:

"There are some people who look a bit like you, but they are
still on the plane. They refuse to get off. They look very scared.
Maybe you can talk to them. They don't seem to understand
anything I say."

So the two women, led by the young pilot, walked across the
hot tarmac and climbed the steep stairs into the cavernous cabin

of the big jet. There, at the very back of the plane, they saw four small figures huddled together, crouching as low as they could in the three seats that they occupied.

My van Tran spoke very gently to them in their own language. She told them who Beatrice was and why she was there, that they had arrived in Australia and that they were very, very safe with the people who were going to look after them. This little family had been living in a refugee camp on a small Indonesian island where the Chinese boatman had left them after a terrifying sea trip from Vietnam. They had been there for three months when the authorities told them to gather their things together as they were going on a plane to another country. They had no idea where. They were very, very frightened, and were all wearing heavy warm clothing as they thought that they may finish up in some freezing part of the world.

Gradually and gently Beatrice and My van Tran were able to lead Hua and his wife, Thui, and their two small children, Tye and Vi, out of the plane and into their car. Their fear and un-certainty were palpable. Hua and Thui clung to their little son and daughter. Beatrice smiled and nodded and offered sweets and small toys. She was desperate to communicate and to make them feel welcome and safe. But her soft-spoken words all had to go through My van Tran. Little by little, the children shyly responded to the sound of her gentle, quiet voice.

Soon they arrived at the YWCA in Mitchell Street, and to save them any more trauma and puzzlement the two women took them through a side door to their new home on the second floor of the hostel where Beatrice had arranged for a small stove to be put in the bedroom and, with My van Tran's help, had bought the foods that she hoped would be suitable for our new guests.

It was several days before the rest of us at the 'Y' saw 'our' little Vietnamese family. They stayed all the time in their bedroom, only talking to Beatrice and My van Tran. They had no idea that they could come out into the garden. They thought that this room was their new 'prison'! At least it was more comfortable and private than their last overcrowded camp on the Indonesian island.

Quickly they all learned some words in English and Hua went off to his job at Paul's Milk Factory. It was a huge success. Beatrice's husband, Graham, was so impressed with him.

"He has a big smile on his face as he is working," Graham said to us, "and he *runs* from the freezer to the truck, to the delivery platform, back to the freezer ...... *all day*! Any more workers where he comes from?"

The story of Hua and his family was such a happy one. One wonders why Australia can't open its doors, and its community hearts, to help the hundreds of desperate people who are still seeking shelter and safety in this huge, affluent and empty land of ours.

After about three months staying with us at the YWCA we were able to find a small house for Hua to rent for his family. They later saved enough money to move to Melbourne and to set up their new lives there. Beatrice, with her quiet and generous manner, had become so important to this special little family that they adopted her as 'grandmother' and she often visited them and remained an important part of their lives until the day she died.

A note from Beatrice to me on my retirement from the 'Y' illustrated for the umpteenth time the double-sided value of voluntary work. She included these words,

'.....*All I can say is a big "Thanks" for helping me personally to want to live again and perhaps be able to enjoy the 'Y' spirit in caring for others'*.

Shakespeare certainly got it right when he had Portia state that:

> '*The quality of mercy is not strained…It is twice blessed:*
> *It blesseth him that gives and him that takes…*'

one of my favourite passages from the *Merchant of Venice*.

TWO MORE STORIES FROM THE 'Y'

Dawn's Story

The Fannie Bay Gaol in Darwin was a basic, very old, small prison set on the limestone cliffs of Fannie Bay. It had been patched up after Cyclone Tracy had battered down all the fences which then, of course, let the existing prisoners run free. (Some of those prisoners had, rather surprisingly, helped to rescue people in the nearby houses where they had been trapped all night in the upstairs remnants of their Cyclone destroyed homes, finding ladders to climb up and help the distressed occupants to climb down through the rubble and shredded bushes.)

But the fences of the prison were quickly restored and the prison population started to be re-established. A small cottage on one side of the prison complex was fenced in for women prisoners. But there was nothing for the women prisoners to do. Most of them were Aboriginal women and the only variation to their day was a visit from a Nun from the Catholic Church to give them Bible lessons, and also of course, being *women* they did the washing for the male prisoners.

The prison authorities sent out a plea to the YWCA for 'someone to come and give some sort of classes to the women'. I passed this request on to the staff and each one of them looked absolutely blank, probably thinking,

"Goodness, there's nothing that *I* can teach them. Not sure I'd want to go into a *prison* anyway".

'*OK*', thought I, '*when all else fails, it falls to the 'boss' to pick up the pieces*'.

I had at least been into the prisons of Papua New Guinea and South East Asia, so I had felt and observed the restrictive and limited world that these people lived in. And I could also use a sewing machine and put together pieces of material to make some sort of garments.

"Perhaps sewing classes for the women?"

Fortunately it happened that the women's section of the prison had a few sewing machines and a couple of boxes of material, so off I set.

This time as I was without Jim to lead the way as in the other countries, it was quite a bit more daunting. I knocked on the first barred door of the Fannie Bay Gaol. Eventually it was opened by a huge prison officer who grunted something at me. I was taken into a small tin office, my bags and pockets emptied, two large books to sign, and then out through another locked door, across a bare yard where men in khaki overalls, obviously prisoners, were wandering aimlessly around, through another locked and barred gate and we approached another high, barbed-wire topped fence, this time with a few bushes growing inside its perimeter.

This fence contained the last barred gate and I was met by the piercing bright blue eyes and quite friendly smile of Mrs Nancy Barham. Nancy was the Chief, and almost only, Prison Officer of the women's section of this ramshackle old prison. She quietly thanked me for coming and led me through a bit of garden into the small neat main room of a very simple tropical cottage. Four Aboriginal women and two white women looked at me with very solemn faces. I wondered if they knew that my husband was one of the two only Judges of the Supreme Court of the Northern

Territory, and if indeed it had been my husband who had put them into this very confined place.

However, there was no indication of any anger or resentment, so we settled down to cut out baby's nightdresses from some plain flannelette material that had been tucked away under the beds in the eight bed dormitory. As we pinned and machined we gradually talked a bit. Mrs Barham watched everyone very closely. At one stage she left the room to speak to an Officer at the barred gate.

"Mrs Barham seems OK", I said tentatively.

"Yeah", said one of the inmates, "she's real tough, but we're lucky, she's also real fair".

And so the three hours went by, and I was released!

As I sank into my car which was parked on the top of the cliffs outside the prison, I let out a huge breath of relief. I hadn't realised how tense I had been while I was 'locked up'. Of course I could leave anytime, but it would still require the unlocking and re-locking of five barred gates by about five different officers. And this set up, apparently, was the only environment, and our sewing class the only women's program that existed in Darwin to punish and straighten up the many misfits and mis-guided people who fell into the Criminal Justice system in our Western World, and, through the rule of Law, were sent to prison with all its limitations and deprivations, for varying extended terms. I could understand why Jim so disliked sending the average offender to prison where, he would say, '*he only learns to be a better crim in there.*'

And so I went back to these women in their locked cottage, week after week, and always with that heavy rock in the pit of my stomach until I was 'released' each time.

On my second visit I became more aware of the older of the two white women. She was practising machining straight lines on a plain piece of material. She was small, very white, blonde straight hair; very sharp, clear light blue eyes. Her name was Dawn.

"Gawd, Mrs Muirhead. I had nightmares about these here machines all week! There was a mob of monkeys riding on these 'orrible machines and they were chasing me down every street. I just gotta get these lines straight they kept yelling at me."

"Never mind, Dawn," I said cheerily, "you won't be in here for long will you. You're only in for shop-lifting I think. It's not as if it was murder or anything like that."

I almost missed the silent and pointed looks that were exchanged between the other women.

A couple of weeks later Jim came home from work and said,

"I had a young woman in Court this morning. Someone who says she knows you."

"How could that possibly be?" I asked.

"Youngish woman called Dawn."

I looked startled.

"She came before me on a charge of murder."

"Oh no" I gasped, "that's not possible. She was only in there for shop-lifting."

"Well, she also has a murder charge pending. Her counsel, Trevor Riley, asked for bail for her as he is positive she is not dangerous. But her bail depends on you, my dear wife."

"What one earth would *I* have to say about such a thing," I bleated.

"It seems that a friend of Dawn's works at the YWCA and is willing to go bail for Dawn and help to keep a very close eye on her. *But* it all depends on you being willing to have her staying at the 'Y' hostel. You do have that grant you told me about from the Department of Community Development to help pay for her board and lodging. Dawn seems to think that you can do *anything*."

And so it happened. Mr Justice James Muirhead QC wrote the order that:

'Ms Dawn S. is to be released on bail on the surety of Mrs Grace C, to live at the YWCA of Darwin, and to obey all the instructions of the Executive Director, Mrs Margaret Muirhead, until such time as a date for a trial is set down.'

So into the 'Y' came our next colourful resident. Dawn was fairly subdued, but very relieved. She had hated prison life and had been really scared of having to go back in again. Of course, a murder charge is a really serious matter and anything could happen, but somehow we didn't think too far into the future. It was enough to keep Dawn away from the Law for these weeks that she would be with us living at the 'Y'.

Mrs Elizabeth Denton, our capable, dour, seemingly old-fashioned Scottish House Manager was amazing. On various occasions she was called out late at night to collect a very drunken Dawn from some noisy, sleazy bar in the City. Dawn, through her alcoholic blur would mutter:

"Gotta stay *every* night at the 'Y'. Judge said I gotta, or that *lovely* Mrs Muirhead will give me back to the cops. You take me home Mrs D. an' I'll be good."

Mrs Denton was so patient with Dawn. She was very firm with her, but she listened to Dawn's story of how her two sons were taken from her because she was drinking too much, so she drank more, and more. And then, running out of money, turned to the streets to collect some dollars as a prostitute.

"And I'm AC/DC—happy to go both ways," Dawn once proudly said to Mrs Denton, whose only sign of shock was a tight clenching of her jaw.

But there was one time when Dawn would not let Mrs Denton be her saviour. In a moment of alcoholic despair Dawn cut her wrists and bled profusely all over the community bathroom at the 'Y'. An ambulance was called and it whisked her down the road to the nearby Darwin Hospital.

Much later in the day I received a call from the Hospital:

"We have Dawn S. here with us but she refuses to sign the admission papers so that we can treat her wounds properly and keep her in hospital for observation. She tells us that *you* are the only person she will talk to."

I raced down to the hospital and found Dawn, covered in blood, still not treated, and refusing to get on the bed for proper attention.

"Dawn, Dawn, what is happening here?" I said.

"Look Mrs M," she slurred at me, "*your* Judge said I have to spend every night at *your* Hostel, otherwise I go back to prison," and then with floods of tears, "I 'ate it in prison...... I gotta be at the 'Y'. Take me back, *please.*"

I managed to calm her down, and I was able to assure her that she had my permission to be in the hospital, and at last I was able to persuade her to sign the admission paper, which she did with a wobbly and slightly bloody 'X'.

Dawn's case eventually came up before none other than Mr Justice Muirhead. So I was able to hear many of the details of the sad and sorry case. It seemed that a group of the 'long grass' people were all so drunk that nobody knew what had happened when one of the men in the group had died with a knife in his chest. They all seemed to point to Dawn because she was the smallest person there and she seemed to be pulling the knife out and trying to put it in her own chest.

"But I stopped shoving it into my belly 'cos it bloody 'urt, that's why," she muttered as she was being questioned.

There was simply no concrete evidence to hang on anyone. The Judge dismissed the case and Dawn was released, returning to the 'Y' after suitable, and rather lengthy celebrations at the bar of the Darwin Hotel. One unpleasant incident marred Dawn's relief. At the bar, where all participants in the case seemed to be drinking, (except the Judge, of course), one of the Police Detectives who had been heavily involved in the case bought a drink for Dawn and with a hard glint in his eye shoved it up the bar towards her. But when she lifted the glass to drink the whiskey and soda, she saw lying in the bottom of the liquid a small, live bullet! She was seriously shaken. She knew that it was a silent way of saying, 'I'll get you yet!'

Jim's attitude was much kinder. He was a bit taken aback, though, one day when he saw Dawn on the street while he was taking his lunchtime walk around Raintree Square in the city of Darwin. She stopped him and said,

"Hi Judge, I guess I owe you one, don't I, eh?"

Jim stepped back a bit and said,

"Don't be silly, Dawn. Don't talk like that!"

"No" she said, "it wouldn't be fair to Mrs Muir'ead would it, and she was real good to me when I stayed at that place of hers."

And a much happier outcome from this tale of woe was the arrival of Dawn at the 'Y' a couple of weeks later, asking to see me. She had a small parcel, which she almost shyly handed to me.

"Just wanna thank you for helping me, Mrs M."

I opened the neatly wrapped package and found a small pendant which was a tiny glass bottle filled with shiny silver filings, and a silver lid holding the filings in place.

"Oh Dawn, that is so pretty," I said, and then unthinkingly and probably uncharitably,

"Oh Dawn, did you nick it?" (shoplifting *had* been her other trade).

"No I never," she exploded, "I 'ad to '*awk the fork* for several nights before I could afford to buy that thing. I just wanted to say thanks."

Of course, I thanked her properly, and to this day, that little pendant has been one of my favourite pieces of jewellery.

Charlie's Story

It was a hot sultry evening in the middle of the Build-up in Darwin. We had just finished our last YWCA Board Meeting for the year and the Senior Staff Member, Margaret Craddock, and I were standing at the open door of the building discussing a couple of the stickier points that had come up during a rather long and trying meeting. Margaret was a strong, down-to-earth woman who had come from the YWCA in New Zealand to help us to get re-established after Cyclone Tracy had sent all our staff, except Miss Rose of course, running for shelter down south. It was nearing midnight and as we were agreeing that it was time for me to move on home and for Margaret to lock up and get to her room, a dark figure emerged hesitantly from the shadows of the street. A young, very dark, Aboriginal man, staggering slightly as he came up to us, moved to walk straight past us and into the building.

Margaret held out a gentle restraining hand:

"Can we do anything for you?" she said.

"I have to see my sister," murmured the young man. "I have trouble."

"And your sister is…?"

"Dorothy. My sister live here. She sleep here. She will help me. I am Charlie, her brother. I will see her."

"Oh, goodness, Charlie," I said, "it is very late. Dorothy is in bed now and she must be up very early tomorrow morning. She is working at the school around the corner. She is learning to be a Teacher's Aide. She works very hard. Can we help you?"

His voice rose a little.

"I have to see my sister. My trouble is bad. My sister will fix it. I *will* see her *now*," and he went to push past us again.

And again, a slightly firmer but still gentle hand from Margaret:

"No Charlie. It is very late. Too late. Come back in the morning to see Dorothy. Come early, before she goes to work."

Charlie stepped back, stood a little taller, and his slightly bloodshot dark liquid eyes flashed startlingly. His voice rose again.

"Yes," he said menacingly, "I will come back. I will come back in the morning. I will have two spears. One for you!" and he pointed a long black finger at Margaret's left eye, "and one for you!" and he pointed the other hand towards my head. Then he turned away from us, strong and tall, and disappeared back into the darkness of the street.

Margaret and I looked at each other and shrugged, quite pleased that we had solved the problem without too much fuss and without any difficulties arising.

I was a little late arriving for work the next morning and Margaret was already sitting in the front office checking the register.

"What on earth has happened to you?" I gasped when I looked at her. Her left eye had a huge purple and black bruise around it.

"Oh dear, silly me," she said, "I was going up the stairs, obviously a bit fast, and I tripped and fell forward, knocking my head on the top step. Somehow my glasses dislodged and caught me just under my eye. Rather colourful, isn't it. Could have been a lot worse though."

"Please take care, we can't afford to be without you just yet," I said as I turned to go up to my office and to attend to the day's pile of letters and a million phone calls.

About 11.30 that morning, just before I was due at a Staff meeting, my head started to throb and jagged lines appeared in the corner of my vision. The pain increased alarmingly and I excused myself from the meeting and managed to find an empty bedroom where I collapsed onto the bed as the black headache took over completely.

In the quiet of the darkened room, a memory of the night before, of a very angry young man, bearing the mysteries and the powers of an ancient, ancient culture, who was thwarted of his urgent needs to see his sister by two middle-aged and ignorant white women came to my aching mind. In his frustration did this young warrior dream of his retribution for our interference, and in his mind, carry the two spears of his culture of mystic dreaming and create Margaret's black eye and this throbbing headache that I was now suffering from?

Or were they simply disconnected coincidences of our busy Western lives…?

AND ORDINARY LIFE GOES ON

Through those fascinating and challenging years at the YWCA of Darwin, and the many activities of our creative groups working in the interests of the United Nations International Women's Year, my social and family life whirled on around me.

We had many new friends in Darwin, both short-term residents and the few people who had chosen Darwin as their permanent home. Fun dinner parties went on into the early hours of the morning, quite often finishing up in the host's tropical luke-warm swimming pool, usually most of us just walking straight in to the pool, clothes and all, wine glass in hand, still enjoying the relaxed company of the interesting mix of people.

The most demanding, exhausting but definitely *fun* dinners were the Gourmet Club Dinners. A small group of friends, five couples, urged on by two genuine Gourmet Cooks, met several times a year for a five or six course meal, prepared entirely by the host and hostess, using unique and elaborate recipes which were then presented for inclusion in our own elite recipe book. Not being a gourmet cook, or much of a cook at all really, I always used a special theme for our dinners. Our very first dinner was named on the Menu, 'Junior Judge's Epicurean Journal.' Jim was aiming to serve 'Strawberries Judicibus' after the first four courses. But the Judicial Strawberries didn't ever quite get to the crystal sweets dishes that I had ready for them as, while Jim was cooking them on a small burner on a side table, pouring flaming brandy all over them with a suitable flourish, he turned suddenly to demonstrate some story he was telling, and the whole pan emptied itself onto the jarrah boards of our dining room floor. The only result was even more hilarity.

It was a very successful evening, but I spent two days in bed recovering from all the stressful preparations.

We had a Japanese dinner, where we all sat on the floor around a low table made from the top of the table tennis board set squarely on two or three bricks. Sake was in plentiful supply, so that it wasn't too far for several of our guests to just lie back on the cushions and pass out for a while.

We had a '*Diner Verte*' when every course was *green*, a bit of a challenge. We had a Sri Lankan dinner, following a lovely trip that Jim and I did to that beautiful island, and a Scottish dinner, though I drew the line at serving haggis. But to support the theme of Scottish culture I borrowed some kilts for Jim to wear. He looked very fine in them, sporran and all, but it caused some shock to our special invited guest (we always invited one other couple to keep the company from becoming boring) when she said gaily as she tweaked at Jim's skirt:

"Let's have a look, Jim. I've always wondered what men wore under their kilts," and there, to her horror, were two furry tennis balls dangling giddily under Jim's kilt, slung there in the toes of the pantyhose that he had wrapped around his middle when he was dressing for the evening, and giggling gleefully as he prepared for just such curiosity.

Our most ambitious effort was the Brindabella Gourmet Dinner. Everyone had to bring camping gear to our Block on the Blackmore River as we knew that no-one would be capable of driving home after the 'Brindabella Buster' cocktail that we were planning to serve to relax people after their seventy kilometre drive. It was definitely a 'black tie' dinner, although the black ties were worn in rather unconventional places. Lace tablecloth and silver candelabra decorated the big old concrete slab that served as the only table at the Block, and a specially built barbecue became the chef's stove for preparing the 'Barbecued Beef and Cumberland Sauce'. It was interesting to watch the next morning as Hansa Patel, our strictly vegetarian Indian member, administered paw-paw skins to the suffering heads of the guests who were still lying paralytically in their tents.

On many weekends there were picnics and brief camping trips to distant waterways, with fascinating wildlife, buffalo, wild pig, wallabies, bandicoots, birds and the odd python, and plenty of dust, providing a very welcome contrast to city life. Occasional entertaining and meeting with VIP's and royalty, Government receptions and dinners at Government House left us no time at all for boredom or thoughts of moving back south.

I was very fortunate in that with Jim's job came full time help in the house for me. In those days it was traditional for a Judge to have on his staff a Tipstaff. This person, according to Jim, was a chap who made sure that the Judge's jabot was straight and that the dandruff was brushed off his shoulders before he walked into Court.

But one of Jim's predecessors, Mr Justice Richard Blackburn, decided that as his wife was required to do an enormous amount of entertaining in the interests of visiting dignitaries and other Judges, it was much more important for her to have help in the house and the kitchen. So this arrangement continued for many years. It made it possible for me to throw all my energies into my work *and* my play, and we had many quite elaborate dinner parties for which I did all the cooking, as well as those 'over-the-top' Gourmet dinners, but with another capable pair of hands to do all the cleaning up afterwards and Jim a very willing helper when he was available, they were occasions that I really enjoyed.

And, of course, family and friends from the South came to stay on a fairly regular basis. They were busy, busy fun-filled days.

So the family wheels kept turning. Bill managed reasonably well with two parents who gave him minimal attention, being so wrapped up in their own lives as they were. But he was not an enthusiastic scholar at Darwin High School and as soon as he could he chose to leave school and, with a bit of help from his Mum, he managed to get an apprenticeship with Stan Kennon in his dusty old junk-filled workshop where Bill learned the trade of Fitting and Machining in a way that my father would have thoroughly approved. Improvisation, creative thinking and problem solving were not on the College theory agenda, but Bill majored at it in Stan's unique old workshop, and under Stan's broad and gentle guidance.

A near fatal fall, riding bareback on a large, frisky horse almost finished Bill's career in Mechanics. His fairly new girl-friend, Margie Lague, whom we hardly knew, was a very keen and capable horse woman. Bill, wanting to impress her but being totally inexperienced in handling a horse, gamely leapt on to Charlie, a large chestnut gelding, who then galloped wildly across the paddock and came to a sudden full stop when he saw a shed and a fence approaching. Bill, of course, fell straight over Charlie's head and landed flat on the ground with a large rusty old gate landing on top of him. He was motionless. Margie rushed to his side, yelling loudly as she did. The owner of the property fortunately heard her, came out to the paddock, took one look at the lifeless body under the rusty gate and flew inside to call an ambulance. Fortunately, with the speed of their arrival and the skills of the ambulance crew, followed by prompt attention of the staff of the Darwin Hospital, Bill eventually regained consciousness, and with the patient and devoted encouragement by this quiet little Margie Lague, he overcame his punctured lung and mild concussion and slowly returned to normality. But, as he felt that he *couldn't really recover completely without Margie beside him,* Bill fairly easily persuaded us to let her come and share his room. They were just eighteen at the time! But this was Darwin, not Adelaide, so why not? They were both shy, reticent young people, and kept very much to themselves, but it was amazing to watch them gradually build up each others' confidence, slowly work through their differences, set up life together and, almost forty years down the track, become the family's Big Success Story.

And in amongst all this busy-ness we had the delight of getting to know our first grandchild, Joshua James. Janet, being young, single and teaching full-time at Darwin High School needed her 'time-out' whenever possible and we were only too happy to have little Joshua be with us when we were available. Gramps and grandson revelled in each other's company, pottering around in the garden together or fossicking in Jim's work shed. By this time we had moved into our permanent Darwin residence in Fannie

Bay, a house that the Government had built for us in place of the ruins of the house that had been allocated to us, but which the Cyclone had completely flattened and demolished, and for which I was secretly very thankful. It was built to our specifications and included a very nice swimming pool. Joshua very quickly learned to swim, although not till after he had been scooped out of the deep end by his watchful grandfather when he was leaning out a bit too far trying to retrieve a funny little boat that he and his 55 year old Gramps had tacked together. Joshua was a very easy, undemanding and happy little boy. We both adored him and considered ourselves very fortunate to be able to have so much to do with his early development, and to enjoy so many happy times with him. Life-long and very close bonds for the three of us were created from those early days.

Then one night in about 1978, quite late, we had a phone call from Richard.

"Mum, Dad! Jane (Cowling) is moving in with me into the Young Street house that I have just bought, and we have just got engaged! Mum, it might be nice if you rang Janie's Mum."

"Oh—er—um, OK, I'll do that. Congratulations anyway."

I was excited. I had met Janie on a couple of occasions but always with a crowd of Richard's friends, so I didn't really know much about her. But he sounded so happy and that was good enough for me. And Jim was pleased that his son was planning to actually get married.

So after a few moments I made the phone call to Adelaide:

"Oh, Joan." I said, "you must have a really wonderful daughter for our rather unconventional son to make a commitment of marriage to her. We are so very happy for them."

Dead silence—then a quivering breath from Joan, and,

"This is the worst thing that has happened to us since Brian's mother died. It's not that we don't *like* Richard—but they can't possibly *live* together until they are married. What can I say to my friends? And I can never visit my daughter in that house. We don't know what to do."

I don't remember any more of the conversation but it did leave me rather flattened—and a bit surprised! Obviously I had forgotten the rigid attitudes of certain parts of Adelaide at that time.

A couple of months later I had the opportunity of going to Adelaide and I stayed with Richard and Jane in Richard's Young Street house. I arrived rather late so didn't have much time for chat before we all went to bed.

But the next morning, after Richard had gone to work, a small elfin figure came into my room and perched on the end of the bed, and talked—and talked. I was fascinated, and completely won over with Janie's enthusiasm, sense of fun, and her interested enquiry into *my* life and *my* activities, and even what my thoughts were on various aspects of life. It was obvious to me that she was highly intelligent, with a slightly mischievous attitude to people and their behaviour, but with a surprising lack of confidence in her own ability. She was most certainly a good challenge for Richard. I imagined that they would have an interesting life together.

Later that year, just after Christmas, Richard and Jane were married at a suitably 'Adelaide' Reception House, with an *un*suitably inebriated bride, weaving her way through the proceedings. Not long after, they moved to live in Perth where Jane had been offered a job as a psychologist in the Health Department of Western Australia. And so began their rocky life together. And they produced our two next wonderful grandchildren.

It was Friday November 28th 1980, the day that I was leaving my job at the Darwin YWCA. After six action packed years as the Executive Director of this rapidly growing organisation I felt that I was running 'out of puff' and that I was not really putting all my energies into all the different projects that we had set up since the Cyclone. I had made the decision to bow out before I had any disapproving fingers pointing at me, keeping in mind a quote from a Chinese philosopher that I had heard at one of the National Executive YWCA meetings,

'... *if you do not resign in time you will not only lose your fame but being unable any longer to perform your duties adequately, you also betray your trust.*'

As I reached my office for *my last day in paid employment*, the phone rang. Expecting another 'good luck on your retirement' call, I was surprised to hear Richard's voice,

"Hey, Mum. How would you like another grandson? Young Timothy James Cowling Muirhead arrived this morning. A month early! Bit of a shock, but he and Janie are both OK!"

So my final day of working at my beloved 'Y' was made perfect by this new knowledge that another precious little person had come into my life, even though it would be a few months before I could actually see and hold him.

STEPPING OUT

Soon after my 'retirement' I gave myself a bonus of going to England for three weeks to visit Tim and his long-term girlfriend, Michele. They had been travelling, working and living together for several years and seemed to be a permanent fixture. They had settled in London with Liz Muirhead, the ex-wife of a cousin of Jim's, and I loved the thought of visiting them both there. Jim was a bit surprised at this rather independent decision of mine, and I think, a little puzzled and maybe even a bit hurt that I could go off, *on my own*, on this venture without even suggesting that I might need him to accompany me. However, he accepted my plans quite well.

But, unfortunately, when I arrived at Liz's four-level rather over-crowded apartment in Earl's Court, there was most definitely an air of tension between the two young people who had been so wonderfully happy when I last saw them before their departure from Australia. It took a couple of weeks, and a few tears, before I was allowed into the dilemma that, as good as the relationship had been for nearly eight years between the two young people, their paths, unhappily, were drifting in opposite directions. So I didn't see too much of either of them for a couple of weeks. Both Tim and Michele were working at full time jobs, and they kept much to themselves in their spare time. So I spent a fair bit of time wandering London on my own and visiting a few friends, including Max and Maartje van der Lecq, a lovely Dutch couple I had met in Greece during a yacht trip that I did after the YWCA World Convention in 1979. I stayed with them in their tiny two-storey terrace house in Holland with their three children, Marjian, Martyn and Marina. They were very kind to me, but with minimal English for them and zero Dutch for me, and a lot of sign language all round, it was a bit of a bi-lingual challenge for all of us.

On my return to London I found that the two sad young people that I had left there were gradually coming to terms with the fact that their lovely relationship had run its course, but it was so very sad to see them both suffering so much, and coming home in the plane I poured out all my heart-ache for them into an ordinary sort of verse that helped me a little to come to terms with my own feelings:

'When she spoke to him he answered, and he used nice simple
  words,
But his answers had no feeling and she wondered if he'd heard.
Even, she hoped he didn't notice that his mother's heart was sad
As their idle chatter faltered to an empty lonely void.

So the fragile wall grew thicker and the atmosphere more bleak
As their contacts were less frequent in the second empty week.
She saw two hearts slowly dying and the pain was felt by all,
But they would not share their burden though all knew the end
  must fall.

So she blundered in and forced them to reveal their private
  pain,
And she prayed for words to help them as they struggled to
  remain
Two civil, caring people who have reached that tragic bend
When joy and love have left them, yet they cannot face the end.

For their love has been so tender, and their friendship so sincere,
But they've passed from youth to adults and they've changed
  from year to year.
It's a mother's saddest burden to see her dear son weep,
And to be withheld from helping brings her almost to defeat.

But with careful, patient loving of the mother, son and friend,
The tattered hearts were severed, and now…May they mend
In the simplest, swiftest manner with new loves and new
  found ways
And new strengths to keep them living through the fullness of
  their days.'

Although Jim was still working full time he seemed to find time for more travel and we travelled together, all over the place. It was on a second trip to Europe in 1982 to visit Tim that we met Annie, Tim's new love, for the first time, and enjoyed getting to know her and were able to appreciate seeing Tim's happiness renewed and their growing interest in each other.

We travelled to Europe and stayed in a tiny snow-covered village in Bavaria for two weeks, enjoying walking in the snow covered woods, and seeing deer and squirrels leaving footprints in the crystal snow. And there, Maartje and Max and their children stayed with us and shared some happy times together, the children practising their English with much delight.

Then late one afternoon we called Richard and Jane from the local Mittelburg Post Office.

"You now have your first granddaughter," Richard shouted through the long distance phone connection. "What shall we call her? Any suggestions?"

"Bavaria," I screamed back, so excited and buoyed up was I.

"Too much like a box of chocolates," Janie chimed in, "how about Hannah?"

The cheery German staff at the Post Office, not knowing much English but hearing the rather Germanic name 'Hannah' smiled broadly and clapped their hands and called out,

"Ya, Ya. Hannah. *Das ist ein guite Deutch name.*"

So Hannah Jane Cowling Muirhead, born on April 12th 1982, came into our lives, giving us the same joy, delight and pride as had the two little boys before her, and an ecstatic Jim fulfilled his promise of '$1,000 to the first grand-*daughter*,' with the hastily added, '*born in wedlock*'.

Then back to Darwin and to the busy-ness, and fun, of our very full lives there. Occasionally we could escape for a hot and dusty weekend at our beloved Brindabella—our block of 20 acres on the Blackmore River, where we had built a wired-in shelter to sleep in, had a wood campfire and barbecue, a few kerosene lanterns, a shovel and a roll of toilet paper. We both loved these weekends, sometimes just the two of us, sometimes with friends or family. Back then we were able to swim in the 40 foot deep water-hole that remained after each Wet Season had almost completely flooded the area, and we would drive out onto the black soil plains nearby and see wild pig, wallaby, buffalo and an occasional brumby amongst the unique magnetic termite mounds dotted on the plains. *Never* a crocodile in those days, but masses of birds and once or twice a large snake. It was the most wonderful place to escape to, breathe deeply of the warm moist air, and revitalise our spirits for the next action-packed weeks.

MY RETIREMENT?

Retirement life in Darwin, for me, was just as busy as my working life had been. I chaired several committees, including a couple of Government ones. I attended conferences, made speeches, well perhaps, *gave talks*, entertained visiting dignitaries, sat on the National Executive of the YWCA of Australia, and the National Executive of the UNAA Status of Women committee, and helped to set up budget accommodation in 'Larrakeya Lodge' which was a combined project of the YWCA and the YMCA. I was very happy to become Chair of that rather large and ambitious enterprise.

This new project was made even more enjoyable by the fact that Adrian Harris, who had been the Executive Director of the YMCA and with whom I had reached a good working relation-ship, had been selected to be the Manager of this large and much needed low cost accommodation. He was extremely capable, very good company, a single father devoted to his two small sons, and still managed to set up and run the 200 bed Lodge and its excellent café with efficiency and good humour. We became very good friends as well as working colleagues, and I have valued that friendship which has lasted through the various dramas of our separate lives, into this present day. And together we proved that the YMCA and the YWCA *could* work harmoniously and profit-ably in the combined management of Larrakeyah Lodge, which was a unique achievement, at least in Australia, for both the 'Y's.

And of course, International Women's Year was still being cel-ebrated with the year 1985 being the end of the Decade for Women, bringing even more celebrations.

Amongst various projects to celebrate the End of the Decade we ran a very simple, but so enlightening computer course for women. To see the young faces of some of the housewives of Darwin light up as they discovered that, by the touch of a button they could arrange a list of names *alphabetically! So easy!*

'Now, I feel a member of the human race again,' and,

'now I might be able to understand what my kids are talking about,'

were excited comments that were often heard from the many participants.

Dame Roma Mitchell, the first woman in Australia to become a Queen's Counsel, a Judge of the Supreme Court and a State Governor, addressed a packed Darwin auditorium. She spoke to us of Women's Rights, but equally passionately of Women's *Responsibilities*.

We ran a Forum on the serious issues of uranium mining, although, at that time, and rather surprisingly, there were more speakers supporting it than condemning it.

We created a multi-cultural theatre performance, 'Women's

Own Work,' for which I wrote the theme song, 'WOW. Equality, Development and Peace,' and we lobbied hard for better recognition of the value of women in the work force and also the work of women in the home.

By now we had our own Women's Advisor to the Chief Minister, and the Northern Territory Government, in keeping with the other State Governments, was really starting to listen to the voices of women, and to include them in more and more aspects of public life. I was still concerned that there was not enough recognition of the work of the woman and mother who chose to stay at home and who took on the role of the full-time carer of her family. I was often dismayed to hear working women, those who received pay for their work, almost denigrating the role that '*the housewife*' played, and I willingly spoke up strongly in support of the home-carer's decision and value. And to my continuing amazement, people seemed to listen and to consider my words.

I was flying high on my community involvement, I was busy every day with committees and meetings, and still our social life kept spinning around us.

Darwin had been very, very good to me.

THE LINDY CHAMBERLAIN TRIAL

Back to Jim's work in Darwin where he grappled with the intense intrusion of the media throughout the long and over-publicised trials of Lindy and Michael Chamberlain following the mysterious disappearance of their baby daughter, Azaria, at Ayers Rock on the 17th of August 1980.

For two years, up to the time of the Supreme Court trial in Darwin in September 1982 in which Jim was the trial Judge, this unusual case had been given enormous worldwide publicity and attention. The cry from Lindy, "*A dingo has taken my baby!*" had echoed around the world. The media painted a macabre picture of a crazed young mother, frustrated by the burden of a nine weeks old baby cramping her camping holiday with her husband and two young sons, had suddenly and inexplicably cut the baby's throat with some camp scissors, hidden the little bloodied body in a camera bag and then made that dramatic cry that resounded throughout the still and mysterious air that will always surround the grand monolith of Uluru, in the heart of Australia's great desert country. No sign of the baby, vague signs of dingo prints, strong denials from the young parents and angry pressure from the police and media made this case one of the more notorious ones in the history of Australia's Criminal Courts.

And for seven long weeks, commencing on September 13th 1982, Jim was responsible for conducting this trial. The whole procedure weighed heavily on him, not because of any complicated details of Law, but the overwhelming publicity and constant media presence that made every word and action from him subject to constant and invasive scrutiny. He became very, very serious.

As the case proceeded he could see that it was possible that there was not enough *factual* evidence to convict either Lindy or her husband, Michael, of being involved in this extraordinary disappearance of their infant daughter. But the media seemed to be baying for blood, and the police produced witnesses from all over the world to prove that the dingo was innocent! But Jim also knew that, in Australia at that time, in the unlikely case of the jury bringing in a verdict of 'guilty' the only sentence that he could pass on this young, and pregnant woman, was '*imprisonment for life!*'

At the end of each long day in Court, Jim would sit on the front veranda of our house in Fannie Bay, surrounded by the colourful crotons and bougainvillea of our tropical garden, and as he sipped his whiskey and drew on his cigarette, he would ponder, often out loud, on the evidence of the day, the behaviour of the various witnesses, and the intensity of the media attention.

"Trial by media, not trial by jury," he would sometimes mutter into the warm, humid air.

All I could think to do in this heavy time was to 'feed the inner man' in any way that I could. His mother's chocolate pudding, sweet curry, sausage and mash and a smiling wife willing to listen and to pour the whiskey, were my only ways of providing some meagre support. And he surprised me later in the trial by saying one evening,

"Thank you for being so nice to me while all this trial has being going on."

At last all the evidence had been heard. The prosecution and defence lawyers had given their closing addresses. Over the next two days Jim read from the one hundred and seventy pages of his long summing up in directions to the jury in which he emphasised the importance of reaching a verdict, only '...*according to evidence, not a verdict based on emotion, sympathy, anger or indignation.*' And further, '...*we are not concerned with questions such as morality, political or religious persuasions...*' and, '.....*we must assess people as they are, and not as we think they should be.*'

The Jury retired to consider the verdict. As it was quite late on a Friday night I went into the Court House and waited in Jim's Chambers for the jury to make their decision.

At about ten o'clock the Judge was called back into Court. The jury had reached a verdict. I went downstairs and slipped into the back of Court Room Number One. It was *packed*, with standing room only. We all stood as the Clerk of Court made three loud knocks on the door from the Judge's Chambers, and the Judge came in to take his position on the Bench, returning the traditional bow of respect, both for the law and the people. The crowd was hushed and expectant. The jury was summoned. One by one they entered the jury box. I was shocked to see that the three women of the jury were quietly sobbing into their handkerchiefs.

Jim then spoke:

"In the case of the Crown against Alice Lynne Chamberlain, how do you find the defendant, guilty or not guilty?"

The foreman of the jury stood up in the front corner of the jury box.

"We find the defendant guilty, Your Honour."

A gasp echoed around the Court Room and stifled sobs could be heard.

And Michael Chamberlain was also found guilty as an accessory.

So the Judge had no alternative but to commit Lindy to life imprisonment, reserving his sentencing of Michael till the next day. And the court was closed amidst high emotional discussions and tensions.

The next morning, the media, in all its fickleness, had huge headlines.

They now seemed to be full of sympathy for 'poor Lindy'… They dwelt on the fact that she was pregnant, that the witnesses were biased, that the sentence was cruel, and so on.

Jim took one look at these comments and sank back into his chair, exhausted and deflated.

"After all that screaming for conviction those bloody journalists completely change their story. What's the good of conducting a full and fair trial for these long seven weeks if the media is going to take over the truth and put forward its own story."

I felt so sad for him.

Just then the phone rang. It was Elva, the head house-maid from the YWCA. She was a genuine, warm person for whom I had respect and affection. She was an older woman who was from the same Church as Lindy and where Michael was the Pastor, the Church of the Seventh Day Adventists.

"Mrs Muirhead," she said in her soft voice, "of course we at the Church are all devastated by what has happened to Lindy, but I have been asked to ring you to say 'thank you' to the Judge for the way he looked after our Lindy through this terrible time. He always spoke kindly to her and the fact that he gave her a comfortable chair and plenty of breaks so she wouldn't be too exhausted, being pregnant and all that, just showed us what a good man he is. Please thank him from all of us at the Church."

I passed this generous message onto Jim but I don't think that it lifted the dark shadow of despair that had overtaken him. The chapter that Jim wrote in his memoir, *A Brief Summing Up*, questioning the values of trial by jury perhaps comes from this first-hand experience of the influence and the persuasion of a biased media.

SECTION 6
A BRIEF RETIREMENT

FIRST ATTEMPT

Then unexpectedly, at the beginning of 1985, Jim said,

"I'm ready to retire. I'm going to be 60 this year. My father died at 66 after retiring at 65. I want to have a bit more retirement time than he had."

"Oh… Where will we retire to?" I said, thinking we couldn't *possibly* leave Darwin.

"Why, Perth of course," said my always decisive husband. "I want four seasons again, and there are no kids left in Adelaide."

"Oh…" said I again, this time a little flatly. I just couldn't imagine what my life would be without Darwin and all my activities throughout the Northern Territory, and also without Janet and Joshua, and Bill and Margie and their lives. I was still very closely involved with the YWCA, both at the National and the local levels. I was probably going to attend the final conference to be held in Kenya for the end of the Decade for IWY later in the year. My social life was giddy, and *fun*. I guess I had become a biggish fish in my smallish pond.

But the decision was made and I knew that I would love being in the same city as little Tim and Hannah, and sharing more closely in their childhood and development. But how I would miss my beloved Joshua. He had been able to spend so much of his first nine years with us, and Jim was a very important figure in his young life.

But changes do happen, and I feared this one almost as much as the unknown mountain that was put in front of me way back in 1974. And of course, for completely opposite reasons. I had come to *love* the Territory and all the colourful, different, warm, friendly, hard-working, fun-loving people, some of whom lived here for just a couple of years and also those who had chosen to make it their permanent home.

'Dragged Screaming to Paradise,' a one-woman play, written by Suzanne Spunner, the wife of the Chief Magistrate, could have been my very own story. Her words so clearly expressed my feelings. And they revealed to me that these feelings were no different from those of many women before me who had come, ever so reluctantly, to this rare and unusual part of Australia, only to be completely won over by its warmth of spirit, its opportunities, friendships, colourful and varied cultures, its intriguing bushland of mysteries and adventures, and its open egalitarianism that so ardently embraced us if we were willing to accept its challenges. How much I had gained from these eleven and a half years in this generous Territory. How much it had changed my whole way of thinking and living. How much I would miss it.

And so the last months of 1985 flew by. Jim was both Acting Chief Justice and Acting Administrator during some of that time. Farewell parties, dinners, ceremonies and presentations were abundant. For some bothersome reason I picked up a fairly serious dose of Hepatitis A, and my energy levels, food and alcohol intake were seriously depleted. Fortunately, though, with the Acting Administrator's job came the services of the Government House staff, including the chef and the driver, so I was able to take part in most of the festivities, but it really was a bit of a struggle for me at times and I sank thankfully onto my bed in any spare moments that I could find.

At last, on September 30th 1985, our departure date had arrived. We were escorted to the small VIP lounge in the over-sized tin shed that was the Darwin Airport Terminal, and fond farewells were made with our beloved Darwin family and a few very close friends. We boarded the plane and sank exhausted into our First Class seats, *probably for the last time*, I thought silently, and we prepared ourselves for the quiet and unknown time ahead of us.

We arrived in Perth in the early evening and were greeted by a most colourful group of young people, our Perth family. Richard and Janie, Tim and Annie, and little Tim and Hannah then five and three years old, met us with big smiles and slightly crazy party costumes. Our spirits lifted immediately. They all seemed really happy to have us arriving to live amongst them all.

As we went out of the Perth Airport building Richard pointed to a huge black car with a uniformed driver standing beside it.

"Looks like someone fairly important is expected" he said.

"Yes, probably," said Jim, delightedly carrying his first little granddaughter and breathing in the cool spring air of Perth.

"Well," said Richard as the other kids gave secret giggles, "we'd better get in it. This car is here for you, Dad and Mum, to take you to your new home in Cottesloe."

What an inspiration that was. Richard in his creative way, and he and Tim being sensitive to the flatness we may feel at leaving all the attentions of Darwin life, had organised this *over the top* welcome for us. Champagne, balloons and streamers, the lot. It was a fun ride to Number 4 Albion Street Cottesloe, lights on in the limousine so that the whole of Perth could see us tossing back champagne and revelling in the company of our generous and thoughtful sons, their wives and our beloved grandchildren.

PERTH

So leaving Darwin and moving to Perth wasn't so bad. Retirement seemed a good idea after all. There was a lot to do in the house and garden in Cottesloe, and also in the house that we had bought in Gracetown the year before. I was still gradually regaining my strength following the hepatitis infection, so Jim had even more to do. But he seemed happy enough.

Our first excitement came from Tim and his fairly new wife, Annie. After travelling happily together from England to Australia they had eventually settled in Perth where Richard and Janie were now living permanently. Mainly to conform to Australian citizenship requirements, (although they *were* genuinely in love), Tim and Annie had married in a very small Registry Office ceremony, attended only by Richard and Janie and their two very small children, Tim and Hannah. So by the time we arrived back in Perth, Annie was several months pregnant. Then on New Year's Eve, 1985, after a fairly raucous and active party at the Gracetown house where we were all staying, Tim woke us very early in the morning of New Year's Day rather urgently saying,

"Mum, Dad, have we any clean towels? Annie's waters have broken. Not sure what to do."

We flew into action. The young parents-to-be set off in their car, first to the Margaret River Hospital, then on to the Bunbury Hospital, and then on the advice of the medical staff there, on to the long journey to King Edward Hospital where Jesse Samuel Muirhead Taylor was safely delivered into this world.

Huge and exhausted relief all round. Jesse, a delightful pixie-faced little boy had arrived a month early, maybe encouraged by the energetic dancing and fun of the celebrations of the New Year in the family holiday house.

Sadly, two or three years later, Tim and Annie's relationship floundered and they called it a day. But, to their credit, they were wise enough to ensure that, in spite of their differences, at all times they took great care to make certain that Jesse did not ever miss out on evenly balanced and caring parenting from each of them. And of course, Jim and I were delighted to have another small person to enjoy in our growing family.

Then in 1986 Jim was asked to go back into the Federal Court in Perth. He agreed. And he hated it. The legal profession in Western Australia were not the slightest bit interested in this 'new' judge who had come from some other part of Australia. The cases he heard had none of the colour and variety of so many of the matters that came before him in the Territory. He was sitting alone, as John Toohey with whom he had expected to share the Bench, had been elevated to the High Court of Australia. Jim had looked forward to working with John again after their years together on the Bench in the Territory. So he was incredibly lonely, and a bit sad.

After six months of this work Jim resigned his commission.

So, more retirement.

But then, at the beginning of 1987, he was invited back to the Territory as an Acting Judge to help to clean up the Civil Lists that contained a long string of cases waiting to be heard.

Now this was a different story. We both jumped at the opportunity to return to Darwin, even for a short time. We found someone to look after the house, our dog Patch, and Maisie the cat, and flew back to Darwin as quickly as we could. It was March, getting towards the end of the Wet Season, and coming down the steps from the plane and walking across the hot tarmac of the Darwin airport, the warm blast of humidity settled down around us, wrapping us in its welcoming arms. It really felt like coming home.

We settled into the Marrakai Apartments in high-rise accommodation provided for us by the Northern Territory Government. Jim loved being back in the familiar, but always respectful, informality and friendliness of the Territory legal profession, and I found a part-time position as book-keeper at the newly relocated YWCA/YMCA project, Larrakeya Lodge. And of course, Janet and Joshua, and Bill and Margie all welcomed us back and made us feel a lovely comfortable part of their lives again.

And a really surprising thing happened to me while we were there. One afternoon I was busily preparing our dinner in the very comfortable two bedroom, two bathroom temporary home on the 10th floor of this quite grand new apartment block when the phone rang. It was someone calling from Canberra, from Government House at Yaralumla! I was a bit puzzled. This man introduced himself and said that he was calling me on behalf of Her Majesty, Queen Elizabeth, who had:

'...*approved the granting of an Order of Australia on me in rec-ognition of the leadership work that I had done in the Territory in support of the women and youth in our community during the past ten years. Was I willing to accept this honour?*'

Ooo...er... my knees went to jelly, my voice seemed to disappear... I took a very, very deep breath and whispered,

"Oh, yes...I think so."

Well, how was that!!! So the past ten years in Darwin in which I had experienced and learned *so* much, where I had worked, often struggled, and had had huge moments of apprehension, anxious sleepless nights, wonderful support from wonderful women, and amazingly successful physical and cultural successes in the community through both the YWCA and International Women's Year, had resulted in the Queen of England, our Queen, saying, more or less, that I had made a bit of a mark and that *she* agreed to it being publicly noted with the awarding of the Medal of the Order of Australia! And all that time it was *me* who was gaining the most, who was discovering that I had some abilities of communication, of being a facilitator, even an organiser, and of bringing out the hidden potential in many women who, like me, thought of themselves as *'just a house-wife!'*. Oh! It left me breathless and slightly stunned.

Jim was most generously excited about this amazing news, and a few days later, at the reception at Government House for the Queen's Birthday, he proudly spread the news amongst our friends who were there.

Soon after this, due to the unacceptable length of the list of cases pending in the Civil Jurisdiction of the Territory, Jim extended his stay in the Territory for an extra three months. Again, of course, I was delighted. By now it was the Dry Season, and we were able to enjoy camps and gatherings at our beloved, dusty old 'camping donga' at Brindabella (fortunately still free of any worries of crocodiles), and we had friends and family visiting us and staying in our luxury accommodation in the Marrakai Apartments. Life was good.

Then, towards the end of August, Jim had a call from the Prime Minister, Bob Hawke.

"Errrrr…Judge," he said, "Bob Hawke here. Errrr… next year is the Bi-centenary of the Founding of Australia." And he went on in words something like this….. 'I've got a few things going, but I reckon we should do something about the Indigenous people of Australia. I worry a bit about reports that I get that a few of these people are dying in police lock-ups and the like. I'm setting up a Royal Commission to look into it. I'm told that you could be the right chap for the job, to be the Royal Commissioner, setting it up and presiding over the running of it. I'd like a result by the end of next year, by December 1988. Errrr…what would you reckon about that, Judge?'

Well, Jim reckoned it sounded good. Anything that may start to lessen the tragedies that he had observed throughout his judicial service in the Territory; anything to lessen the over-representation of Aboriginal people, especially the youth who were so often picked up by the police and locked up for petty crimes; anything to address the complete uselessness of the prison system in making any difference to their behaviour, would be well worth working for.

"It should be an interesting job," Jim said to me, "probably take about nine months. I like to think that I may be able to make some little difference. I would like to say yes to Bob."

"Why, of course," I replied, happy that he wanted to keep working for a bit longer, that he wasn't *really* going to retire just yet to a life of possible boredom.

And then he said,

"And for that time, we'll live in Canberra of course. This is a Federal matter. The Commission will operate from Canberra."

Oh... Once again the balloon burst with a dull plop.

"You mean we both leave the little kids in Perth and go and live in *Canberra* again?"

"Yes, Sweetie, of course! I couldn't do it without you there, and it is only for nine months this time."

Small comfort, but quite nice to be needed, I guessed.

It all happened quite quickly. The young man in our house in Cottesloe agreed to stay on to look after the cat and the garden. We packed up a few things—mostly warm clothes, and our little Cocker Spaniel, Patch—and settled into a rented house, with rented furniture, in Mawson, a newish suburb in Canberra. The house looked straight out at the beautiful mountain ranges of the Brindabellas.

Thankfully, the Butler family were still there in full strength, and shared their warm hospitality to help us to settle in again to this manicured, rather artificial, Australian Capital Territory.

BLACK DEATHS IN CUSTODY

Things for Jim got moving very quickly this time, much quicker than when he took up the job of setting up the Australian Institute of Criminology way back in 1973. Bob Hawke could certainly *get things done* when he had his heart in it. Premises, staff, legal officers, intense schedules, radio and television publicity, interviews, the lot. Jim was on the road again… and Patch and I sat and looked at each other thinking, now what shall we do? Someone had suggested to me that perhaps I should do some sort of a correspondence course to keep me occupied, and although study had never been a favourite activity of mine, it was certainly something to think about. So I enrolled in a course of book-keeping, called rather grandly 'Accountancy One,' and also Business English. Both subjects were challenging, but also surprisingly interesting. They kept me quite happily occupied in the long hours that Jim was away from home during the very demanding days of conducting the heavy and all consuming business of the Commission. And I was quite surprised at the good feed-back that I received from my two tutors for each of my subjects.

Of course, I was involved in many aspects of the side activities of the Commission, and had the privilege of attending the opening sitting in Canberra at which Jim had refused to have any police presence, even though advised that it would be necessary. His view was that there would more likely be trouble if police *were* in sight. He was right. Apart from a disciplined protest from Michael Mansell, an Aboriginal activist from Tasmania, the crowded courtroom showed respect, and I think some appreciation, for the honest and simple terms in which Jim presented the work ahead and the aims of the Commission.

But there was *so* much to be done. Very quickly it was revealed that, rather than the *few* cases of Aboriginal deaths in custody that Mr Hawke had envisaged, there were well over 125. To do the job thoroughly, and he would do no less, Jim knew that the Inquiry could take years, and the Prime Minister wanted a full report by the end of 1988!

Eventually, at a Symposium in Sydney at which he was a speaker amongst several key politicians and academics, Jim, unusually for him, insisted that he be the first to speak. He knew that the journalists and media representatives would only wait to hear a couple of speakers before they raced off to lodge their copy, each with their own particular version of events that they would pass on to their own particular paper, radio or TV station.

And then Jim, the Commissioner of the Inquiry into the Black Deaths in Custody spoke... with stirring passion. He spoke of the growing numbers of deaths, the cultural tragedies caused by the ignorance and lack of educated care by white authority, the uselessness of finding solutions to this on-going tragedy unless *'the underlying causes of the over-population in prisons of Indigenous people were thoroughly investigated'*, and he made it very clear that the Inquiry could continue for at least another decade unless more Commissioners were appointed to spread the load right across the country. And most strongly of all:

'In the International World, Australia will wear the shame of this neglect, ignorance and lack of action.'

These were headlines that the Government could not ignore. As a direct result of this appeal, three more Commissioners were appointed, the cases were divided geographically, Jim was able to centre himself in Perth in a well-staffed office there, and we were able to leave Canberra for good and move back into our little house in Cottesloe, and again be close to our grandchildren and their parents.

But it was a heavy, heavy burden that Jim carried every day as he presided over the Inquiry throughout Western Australia, and still oversaw the work of the other Commissioners. Far from the 'interesting exercise' that he had anticipated when he was first asked to take on the Commission, every day brought more evidence of the destruction of an ancient people's culture, their language, their family structure, their dignity, their health and in many cases, their survival. Could he make *any* contribution at all towards alleviating and changing this slow, callous and ignorant destruction, or would this very public exposure to such close scrutiny make the whole condition much worse for the present survivors? He became quieter and quieter. I think his heart was slowly breaking.

But he met some wonderful people and had very supportive staff. In Western Australia, Norm Harris, his Aboriginal Field Officer, and Pat Dodson, later an Aboriginal Commissioner, helped to bridge some of the cultural chasms. Communities that he visited had opportunities to sit down with him in remote places and tell him their stories. He was never in a hurry in these places. Respect for his single minded attention, and appreciation for his integrity grew, and even the members of the press, known for their fickleness and often negative bias, gave him reasonably favourable and accurate press cover. This, I think, was largely due to the fact that he never, ever, refused an interview, or a phone call, and he was *always* courteous and as open as legally possible.

Just once, this openness backfired. He had, in good faith, allowed a posse of press reporters and photographers into a prolonged inquiry in the Court of Albany. I was surprised to see the cameramen roaming freely all over the courthouse, and trailing Jim and his staff as they went about their personal lives, including a visit to an Aboriginal women's craft centre. It seemed that a really good report might come out of this. And yet far from showing anything positive, such as the great work at the women's craft centre, the resulting TV documentary, seemed determined to misrepresent the truth.

The worst feature was that they twisted Jim's response to two letters he was shown. One was a letter from his Minister, to which he replied, "Yes, I'd have to agree with that." The other was a letter criticizing aspects of the Royal Commission, and his response was, "You know I can't comment on that."

The final program was edited in such a way that, when shown the letter of criticism, Jim's response appeared to be "Yes I'd have to agree with that," thus making him seem, quite wrongly, to be critical of his Minister. Jim was very distressed by this betrayal, although when he rang his Minister to try to set the record straight, that weary man said,

"Don't worry, Jim, this happens to us over and over again. Please ignore it."

And so the Commission dragged on.

In March of 1988 I took a quick trip back to the Territory. Bill and Margie were due to have their first baby. Here was the perfect opportunity for me to be able, for the first time, to be close to a grandchild very soon after its arrival. Margie was due for a Caesarean section, so we could be sure of the date. On the appointed day, Bill and Margie set off from their little house in Freshwater Drive for the Darwin Hospital, and, beset with impatience, I was close behind them, in my hired car. It wasn't too long a wait before Bill, heavily capped and gowned and a bit pink in the face, came out of the operating theatre to tell me that:

"It's a BOY! It is all just amazing, a bit gruesome at times. But he's coming out in a humid crib in a minute."

And there I was, able to greet my grandson, *almost* the minute he was born.

The nurse wheeled him down to the nursery and invited me to tag along. Only too willingly I stayed very close to this tiny pink bundle, and he and I were left alone while the nurse went off on some other busy errand. That little treasure had various tubes stuck to him and looked pretty disturbed by his new surroundings, so I sneakily opened one of the plastic trapdoors that kept him away from the outside 'pollution' and held his tiny little hand. Miraculously, his pathetic little cries gradually quietened, and we just stayed there together, with all my heartfelt love flowing down through my fingers into his.

Later that night my feelings of those most precious moments became these lines:

To Christopher, from Granny.   *March 11 1988*

Your life was carefully planned and very much desired,
Your Mum and Dad both longing for your birth.
You may have been a boy or girl, they didn't really mind,
As long as you came safely to this Earth   .

When Mummy went to hospital your Daddy stood close by;
They both were there to meet your first small cry.
They marvelled at the miracle of your tiny face and hands.
They held you gently with a most contented sigh.

Your Granny waited anxiously till Daddy came and said:
'It's a boy! He's fine! He's wonderful! So small.'
And Mummy smiled, a little tired, it was hard work you see.
But this tiny you, this perfect frame, had made it all worth
    while.

While doctors tidied Mummy up, and Daddy held her hand

The nurses brought you out for me to see.
We went downstairs together, your feet in tiny bands,
I sang you songs, so soft, so quietly.

* * *

Christopher,
Your life lies out before you, for many, many years,
You'll have your share of problems, there may often be some
  tears.
But with parents who so love you and who give each other
  care,
I know that you'll be happy, and you'll find much joy to share.'

So now we had five Grandchildren. Christopher Graham Muirhead was added to our growing family. How lucky can you be!

But the Royal Commission continued to dominate our lives. And Jim's heart grew heavier and heavier. Whereas in the Territory the racial attitudes towards Aboriginal people seemed generally reasonably balanced and well-informed, although there was still a lot of ignorance and bias, Jim found that in Western Australia there was a very different feeling. It had been thought that Queensland carried the worst statistics for the incarceration and treatment of Aboriginal offenders, and for ignorant racism, but it was soon clear that the number of deaths in custody was much higher in Western Australia. And the general attitudes, in this State, towards the first people of this country were negative, and at times quite hostile. Certainly there was heavy intolerance, to say the least. There were rumours that the Western Australian Police were taking out an injunction to stop Jim sitting in WA, and that the prison officers at the Fremantle Jail were seeking counselling to help them cope with any possible involvement they may be subjected to in the Inquiry.

However, with the support of his dedicated staff, and assistance from Justice Dan O'Dea, Jim pressed on with the many, many cases to be heard. Time was moving on, and the Prime Minister had wanted a report before the end of the year of the Bi-Centenary!

THE NT JOB

Towards the end of that year, 1988, Jim and I were having a few days break at our little Gracetown house that we had bought in 1984. We were gazing out over the endless, sparkling blue of the Indian Ocean to the far, far distant horizon beyond which lay Mauritius, the Maldives and South Africa, when the owner of the one and only store of that tiny township drove up in his car. He had an urgent message for Jim to ring Marshall Perron, the Chief Minister of the Northern Territory.

"Oh dear," muttered Jim as he dragged himself up to answer this surprise call. "I hope this isn't another batch of deaths in the Territory. We have a comparatively clean record there so far."

He paused, and stared glumly out over the peaceful beauty that surrounded us.

"I don't think I will ever see the end of this Inquiry. What we have done to the people of this country who have lived here so well for so many thousands of years! We have torn their culture to shreds. Can *anything* we do ever repair it?"

And with that he gathered a handful of coins off the kitchen shelf and went down to the one and only phone box that was the communication point for most of the locals.

He was away for quite a while and, although I tried to concentrate on the cross stitch embroidery that had filled a lot of my 'waiting time' during this past long year, I started to get anxious about the shape and the size of the problem that had come up this time.

At last the car came down our very steep driveway, and Jim's heavy footsteps could be heard clapping up the wooden stairs. His expression was inscrutable. And I waited, again.

"Well," he said as he lit a cigarette and leant over the balcony. "That was a bit of a surprise. The Chief Minister wants me, us, to come back to Darwin, to Government House, to take up the position of Administrator of The Northern Territory. Of course, I can't do it. This Commission will go on for ever. But I am so tired. I sometimes wonder if I have the energy, and the strength, to continue with this seemingly futile, heavy, heart-breaking work."

So, as the sun was sinking in all its golden glory into the darkening ocean, Jim poured us a drink and we talked for a long time about what 'might have been'. Neither of us felt very cheery that night.

Back in Perth, Jim received a call from the Prime Minister. He had also been approached by Marshall Perron regarding the possibility of Jim taking up the position of Administrator of the Territory. The Prime Minister had also had a hint from Jim that 'he was running flat,' and that with the extension of the work to be covered by four more Commissioners Jim thought that the new energy of Elliot Johnson could lift the pace of action and hasten results. Bob Hawke was understanding of this attitude, but he asked that Jim put in his Interim Report before he took 'retirement'. He even suggested that Jim give some thought to the offer from the Northern Territory, but to keep it strictly to himself for the time being.

So with an almighty effort and the support of his staff, Jim was able to complete his Interim Report, with 56 recommendations,

and he presented it to the Government at the end of December
1988. He agreed to work on until May 1989, helping with the
hearings in WA, and nothing more was said about the 'NT Job'.

In January 1989, Jim was in Canberra attending to Commission business, and I was at home, preparing to join him for a few
days. I had started keeping a diary, to cover these tortuous days,
and my entry on Thursday January 12th 1989 is this:

> *Just starting to think about packing my gear to join Jim in
> Canberra tomorrow. Then the telephone call that changed my
> life ... again.*
>
> *"Could I speak to Mr James Muirhead, please?"*
>
> *"No, I'm sorry, he is not in at present. Could I take a message
> for him?"*
>
> *"It is very important that I speak to him. Where can I contact
> him, please?"*
>
> *"I'm sorry. He is in Canberra. Can I ask the nature of your
> ringing?"*
>
> *Then, expecting some further digging and delving from an
> enthusiastic reporter into the convolutions of the Aboriginal
> Deaths in Custody Inquiry,*
>
> *I heard these amazing words...*
>
> *"The Prime Minister has just issued a statement, Nationally,
> that Mr Muirhead is leaving the Commission and will become
> the next Administrator of the Northern Territory."*
>
> *"Oooohaaahooh," said I...*

A little later there was a rather stern phone call from Tim:

"Mother, is there something that you haven't told me?"

Oh, whoops. But when the Prime Minister of the country
tells you that something is confidential that is where it stays, and,
of course, all the kids were equally surprised at the sudden turn of

the life style of their parents that they had, like Tim, first heard on the radio. They received the news with mixed feelings. Jim said he would only do the job for two years, so we would be back in Perth in no time. It turned out that that was *half* true.

A further diary entry.......

'It was good to find that the media treated Jim very fairly about the change of job. Very little criticism. It would seem that he has done such an excellent and balanced, productive and pragmatic job that there is little room for criticism. No wonder he has been so totally immersed and absorbed in thought and rumination over the past 15 months.'

In Canberra we escaped up into the beautiful Snowy Mountains, covered in their summer wildflower glory, and talked and talked. I think Jim could see that he would now survive for a few more years without the full weight of the Inquiry that was visibly and rapidly draining his health from him. It was a lovely time in our lives. We seemed to agree on everything; the joy of being back with old friends in Darwin; the delight of seeing more of Joshua and Christopher, and of course their parents; the thrill of living at Government House and all that went with it; but also the sadness of leaving our Perth families and the Cottesloe house that we had both become quite fond of. And Jim looked, and acted, 10 years younger than he had in the last few months.

The next five months were action packed preparing for this unknown lifestyle to begin. Jim completed his time with the Commission and I spent time organising an improvement to my wardrobe, not something that I enjoyed overmuch, as dress style had never been a skill of mine. I was helped considerably by Nina Boydell, a friend of the boys, who had studied *haute couture* in Italy, and who created some delicious clothes for me. I found a young single mother, who Richard and Jane knew, to come in and be 'caretaker' of our house and garden at a nominal rent. The Official Secretary of Government House in the Territory paid us a visit to brief us on various aspects of what the job involved. I think that made me more nervous than ever. And again, there were farewells and kind words from various friends and acquaintances.

Then on Friday June 30, with very mixed feelings, with several bags of luggage, a cat and a dog, and an armful of flowers, we were packed into two big white cars and taken to the VIP lounge at Perth Airport.

Back to the diary......

'Sitting together in the almost hallowed private lounge we were both feeling a bit blank when in came Annie and Jesse. That saved the day. It was so good to have them both there, although the three and a half year old Jesse behaved rather badly, ignoring all the importance of the place and sitting on the floor and seeing how far he could spit!'

We were all driven out to the middle of the tarmac to a RAAF jet that was waiting for us. And fortunately, the sight of this noisy, big, shiny silver plane filled Jesse with sobering wonder and his behaviour became exemplary. Big hugs and kisses from the two young ones and we climbed up the stairs to saluting staff and a well set up cabin, *just for us*! So this was a taste of the new life! Two large swivelling armchairs half filled the cabin, a blue mohair rug was spread on the floor, with Patch curled up asleep in the middle of it, and Maisie looking very happy on a soft rug in the larger cage that the dog had travelled in from Cottesloe.

We settled back to enjoy lobster and champagne, followed by cheese and Port, and a bit of a chat to the smartly uniformed RAAF officers who were looking after us. It still felt very strange.

At last we circled over Darwin and the big plane came gently in to land. I felt that I was in some grand film as I followed Jim out of the plane and down the steps to be greeted by the VIP's of Darwin, the RAAF Group Captain, Chief Minister, Chief Justice, Lord Mayor and their wives of course, and then also in the line up, to my delight, were the Darwin kids, Joshua, Janet, Margie, Bill and Christopher.

Diary entry:

> *Jim inspected the Guard of Honour and we all stood and looked stunned. Then into the white cars, a bit of a scuffle as Janet and Joshua got into our car... and they weren't meant to!... (who cares)... and off we went to The Sheraton Hotel.'*

Jim was not being sworn in as Administrator until Saturday July 1st so he did not want to occupy Government House until he was officially entitled to. At the Sheraton we were greeted by a *red carpet*, and the manager and Letty Lopez, his wife, with a huge sheaf of flowers for me, and then they escorted us up to the *Royal Suite*! My childhood dreams of being a Princess were almost coming true. We had a wonderful evening, a special dinner with silver service, and Joshua and Chris up to their ears in a huge bubble bath.

Diary entry:

> *'It was magnificent!! More flowers, and a FAX from Richard... wonderfully typical of him to be using up-to-the-minute technical facilities.'*

Saturday 1st July is Self Government Day in the Northern Territory, and this was also the day that Jim would be sworn in as the new Administrator of the Northern Territory. We were taken in the big white car through the gates of Government House, round the circular drive, past the palms, under the scarlet bougainvillea to the steps of our new home. Another red carpet, and there, lined up on the veranda, were the House Staff looking very formal and very nervous. Jimmie Farrell, the House Manager, was first in the line. I had got to know him a bit through the 'International Evenings', the major YWCA fund-raising functions that we had held at Government House in past years, when Jimmie had done everything he possibly could to help us to create a warm, exotic and welcoming atmosphere for these wonderful, colourful displays of the best that the multicultural communities of Darwin could produce in food, dance and brilliant national costumes on the expansive terrace and lawns in the Government House grounds. He was a kind and gentle man, and he was always eager to be helpful and friendly.

After Jimmie had introduced the new Administrator to the line-up of nervous looking staff members, then it was my turn, and I just took his hand and with a big smile, (it was so good to see a familiar face), gave him a big kiss on the cheek, and as he introduced me to the housekeeper, the chef, the housemaids, handyman, laundry maid and gardeners I felt a little of the stiffness melt out of these nine people who were waiting in some apprehension to see what this new 'mistress' would be like to work for.

This first day was action packed. A brief and very formal ceremony, conducted by the Chief Justice in the spacious Drawing Room, followed by the signing of papers, ensured that Jim was correctly sworn in as The Administrator of the Northern Territory, and as I was his wife I was now the First Lady of the Territory. (*Oh my hat.*)

There was a small reception held on the wide veranda of the historic old House, and then we were shown through to the Administrator's Private Apartment. This was a post Cyclone add-on at the back of the four big main rooms that make up the Official part of Government House. This apartment, consisting of three bedrooms, two bathrooms, a study, kitchen, dining-room and separate lounge, all fully air-conditioned with big windows looking out over the Arafura Sea, was to be our home for the next two years. It all felt pretty good.

The Staff had prepared a small family lunch for us. Unfortunately, only Janet and Joshua were at these procedures as, according to my diary:

> *Janet and Bill had had a furious argument. Janet had broken some of Bill's louvres… Bill threw his (never to be found again) keys at her, and general emotional chaos reigned. A diplomatic phone call from Mother gradually calmed things down, and later, Bill, Margie and Christopher, and Patch and Maisie, who had stayed overnight with them, came trotting around the back to our private veranda.'*

We were then taken to the very formal Flag Raising Ceremony… I was horribly nervous. How did I look? Would my hat blow off? Will I walk in the wrong direction? etc etc. Maybe being a princess wasn't quite so much fun after all. Jim inspected the guard, seemingly a very important and regular duty of Administrators and Governors, and two soldiers fainted! In the assembled crowd, it was good to see a few familiar faces, particularly the very broadly smiling face of Nobby Lague, Margie's Dad, resplendent in white shirt and black bow tie, looking as proud as Punch, as if to say:

> *'That chap up there is as good as related to me.'*

Back to Government House where a Senior Staff Member from the Office, Zoe Marcham, and Dick Wallace were being married under the official flag that was flown from the tall flag-pole mounted in the centre of the front lawn. More introductions, handshakes and a couple of kisses, then quickly back to the smart white car, number plate NT1, Australian flag flying proudly on the front of the bonnet, to attend the official Government welcome reception.

Diary entry:

'And that was wonderful... especially for me. I didn't have to make a speech. The Chief Minister's wife, Cherry Perron, accompanied me one way around the crowded room, and Jim went the other with Marshall Perron, the Chief Minister. There were so many people that I knew, and they were so warm and friendly. So many kisses, and a number of hugs. So informal. What a welcome. Marshall spoke very warmly, of both of us. Jim replied, very good as always, sincere, amusing, so unaffected and natural. More greetings. And again, Margie's Mum and Dad were there.'

And so began the most exciting, action-packed, satisfying and happy three and a half years, (and yes, of course Jim extended after the first eighteen months), of our married life.

Highlights? Far too many to include here. Busy? Sometimes too busy to even see our grandchildren, and not much time even for our children. Visitors? A passing parade of friends, relatives and VIP's stayed in the elegant State Rooms. Receptions, official dinners and luncheons for visiting dignitaries, courtesy calls from foreign Ambassadors and their wives, fund-raising functions and ceremonies for community organisations on the huge paved terrace overlooking the Port of Darwin.

We introduced a new initiative at the House. We held Open Day events where the public could wander through the well-cared for tropical gardens and the four State Rooms of this beautiful old seven-gabled Residence, surrounded by its 12 foot wide, louvred veranda, that had withstood the Japanese bombs of 1942, and the devastating Cyclone Tracy of 1974. And the Darwin people from all walks of life came and enjoyed, examined and admired this old house that sat proudly on a high promontory overlooking the Darwin Harbour. It seemed a very popular move.

The staff were wonderful, and never complained at the amount of work that we seemed to generate for them. It was a part of my job to meet with Jimmie Farrell, the House Manager, and Alison, the Housekeeper, a couple of times a week, to plan the forthcoming events to be held at The House, and any staff problems that they thought I should know about. I also met with the Chef at the beginning of each week to plan our menu for the week, including all our lunches and dinners, both private and official. These meetings made me feel as if I was back at the 'Y' again, sorting out problems of personality clashes, and disagreements, smoothing ruffled feathers, and giving well deserved encouragement and appreciation of the wonderful job that they all accomplished. I just loved it.

Jim and I had an early slight difference of opinion about our food. Our apartment was completely self-contained, including a well equipped kitchen. But in spite of that the Chef would cook our dinner in her big kitchen, serve it on two plates, cover each with Gladwrap, and then all I had to do was simply put them in the Microwave oven, and *Presto!* there was dinner.

"Just leave the dirty dishes and leftovers out in the scullery," were the Chef's instructions to me. What a great idea! Along with having the apartment cleaned every day, the beds made every day, all washing, ironing and shopping done by staff, this was definitely the life for me.

But, sadly, that was not Jim's idea of domestic life.

"I do *not* want my dinner to come straight out of a microwave every night," he said. "I want *you* to cook my dinner like you always have!"

Oh dear. And *bother*. I had rather liked this luxurious regime. I spoke to the Chef, and being a good diplomatic person, she suggested that she would prepare the vegetables, create the meat or fish into whatever I had ordered and leave it in the big kitchen fridge. Then I could take the pots and pans into our little kitchen and rattle saucepans and frying pans in the usual manner on my stove, and present *my* meal to my esteemed husband in the way that made him feel *normal*. It worked well, and we were all happy. And Jim usually washed up anyway, as he hated to be 'a bother to the staff,' so there weren't even dirty dishes in the scullery.

It was such a privileged time in our lives. We saw so much of the Territory, and always in the comfort of an air-conditioned car, a small jet, or often a helicopter. We visited remote stations and met wonderful women and men, living isolated lives, great distances even from their children. We visited Aboriginal communities in their home lands. We learnt so much from their acceptance of us. Special corroborees were held for us. We attended a traditional funeral on Bathurst Island, combining both the tribal dancing, the wailing, the smoking and the ashes covering their almost bare bodies, and the Christian formalities adapted to respect the ancient and the modern beliefs of our two such different cultures. Jim conducted an investiture at Milingimbi. Warriors painted with their traditional designs slowly danced the honoured woman up to the Administrator to accept the Award that she was receiving in the Australian Honours system, and an Aboriginal choir of women, dressed in spotless white dresses sang a hymn with the words, 'Jesus, wash me clean.'

(Jim whispered to me, *'they couldn't be cleaner whatever Jesus did.'*)

I particularly enjoyed the 'courtesy calls', when a foreign Ambassador and his wife, visiting Darwin from their home country or from Canberra, made an official visit to Government House to 'call on the Administrator'. Jim always received the couple on the wide veranda that looked out over the sparkling Arafura Sea framed by the brilliant red flowers of the poinciana tree and the softer white flowers of the dark green-leafed frangipani trees. Often a Torres Straight Island Pigeon would be cooing softly in the high branches adding to the perfect tropical setting.

It was my job to entertain the wife while the Administrator and the Ambassador talked diplomatic matters. Often she and I had no language in common, but it was amazing how hand signs, a few simple words and perhaps a brief stroll in the garden kept us both interested in learning from each other, and usually parting with a warm embrace.

I was able to host luncheons for women from all walks of life in the Territory. My wonderful staff and supporters from the YWCA were the first guests on my list. Then I held luncheons for volunteers from the many community groups in Darwin, women who had lived in Darwin for many years, quietly contributing to the well-being of their community, all women who had never set foot in Government House before. They were thrilled, and I loved every minute of it. And who wouldn't! A friendly and enthusiastic staff to do all the preparation, cooking, caring and cleaning up! And lunch was usually followed by a tour through the other three rooms and the wide verandas of this old historic house, conducted by the ever cheerful and justly proud Jimmie Farrell.

A *huge* highlight for me was an invitation issued to all the Governors and Administrators of Australia and her Territories, *and* their wives, just twenty of us, to attend a dinner in Sydney, hosted by none other than *Her Majesty Queen Elizabeth II and the Duke of Edinburgh.*

Oh my! Was I nervous! I had met the Queen on two previous occasions. The first was in Darwin soon after the Cyclone when she and the Duke came to offer sympathy and support following the devastation by Cyclone Tracy. On that formal line-up, meeting the Queen for the first time, I presented my deepest curtsy, (Jim said later that he thought I had fainted!), but the Queen's hand was strong and firm and helped me to return safely to my full five foot one and a half inches height. I was totally overwhelmed and couldn't squeak a word. The second meeting was at the Investiture in 1988, held at Government House in Perth, marking the Bi-Centenary of the founding (or fouling?) of Australia, when the Queen presented me with my little Medal of the Order of Australia. On this occasion I seemed to have plenty to say. Richard and Tim who were in the audience said later that I 'simply wouldn't let the poor woman *go!*' But she seemed so interested that I came from the Northern Territory, and I just *had* to throw in that 'my husband was in the middle of the Inquiry into the Aboriginal Deaths in Custody.'

"Ah yes," said this amazing woman who had fascinated me since childhood when I kept detailed scrapbooks of her every move, together with her sister, the ill-fated Princess Margaret, "we have been following that with great interest."

So here we were at this illustrious Dinner, *chatting* casually with the woman who I had admired and respected from afar for my whole life. Well, *I* didn't actually chat. Jim was such a natural and relaxed conversationalist that I didn't need to. He and the Queen seemed to just be yarning about any old thing. Then the butler came up to Her Majesty and murmured that, "Dinner is served, Ma'am," and she said, "Oh dear, now how shall we do this," raised her arm and called, "Come along now, everyone, dinner is ready for us. All come into the dining room." And there we were, just a handful of people, *dining with the Queen!* What an unbelievable experience for that small, 'un-noticed' little girl who started her life as the youngest and quietest scrap in a large, boisterous family in Adelaide, way back in 1926.

At Government House we entertained other members of royalty, but not any from the British Isles. The King and Queen of Nepal, charming and quiet, but so friendly and dignified, spent a couple of hours with us on their stopover to Canberra. But tragically, soon after their visit they were to be shot out of existence by a crazed member of their family. The Princess of Thailand, with a strange mouth deformity and staff who kow-towed backwards out of her presence, was an interesting visitor, and the Crown Prince of Spain, young, just twenty-one, earnest, and very tall, was a delightful guest at a luncheon on the wide veranda of this historic old House where we were now living. The members of the Darwin Spanish community were delighted to have such an opportunity to meet and talk with him.

So almost every day, and often the evenings too, were filled with interesting activities; dinners, receptions, balls; art exhibitions to be opened, schools to be visited, and speeches at almost every function. Of course, Jim made the speeches, and they rolled off his tongue with seeming ease. But occasionally it was my duty to be the at the podium, and much to my surprise I found that I managed quite well.

I would spend quite a bit of time checking my subject and writing out what I wanted to say. I would try to memorise the beginning and the closing words of what I had written, then, a big deep breath, a reminder to myself that, '*all these people really want to hear what you have to say, they really like you, and you just really love them*' and off I would go. And on most occasions it went surprisingly well. Only then would I let the secretary type out the words that I had written. I was never confident enough to let *anyone* see what I was planning to say.

And, somewhere, in amongst all this public life there was still a little time for family. And the family kept growing.

On Christmas Eve, 1990, little Julia Hamilton came quietly

into Bill and Margie's lives, and we were able to have a large family gathering with the Lagues at Government House to mark her Christening. And in 1992 Janet added a husband, Nick Thomas, to her life, celebrating their marriage in the gardens and verandas of the house of the Seven Gables. Also, Tim became engaged to his second wife, Sue Clear, so there was the promise of another daughter-in-law at the end of that year. On February 4th, 1990, Jim made a big splash of our 40th Wedding Anniversary by surprising me, both with a brunch for a group of our special Darwin friends at the Beaufort Hotel, and even better, the surprise arrival of Tim and Richard from Perth, just for the occasion. That man certainly knew what made his wife happy, and this was a very, very happy weekend. Tim marked it with a fun poem. He possibly summed up my life to this point in a much more interesting, and certainly much briefer way than these lengthy rambling pages that I have muddled through. Richard and a friend of Janet's also performed for us all.

To mark the occasion, Jim gave me a beautiful little bracelet, 'rubies for the 40th, gold for the 50th and diamonds for the 60th,' he said, 'so don't expect any more of these.' Sadly, they were prophetic words.

It was while we were at Government House that, sadly, Richard and Jane's marriage came to an end. In 1990 they had moved to London with Tim and Hannah, aged ten and eight. Richard had been given the rather prestigious job of working at West Australia House as the WA Director of Investment and Trade in Europe. I visited them towards the end of 1991, but felt a certain unease and lack of the usual high spirits that always existed in their family life, although we did have a wonderful long weekend in France, staying in a '*gît*' to celebrate my 65th birthday and making a more sobering visit to the War Cemeteries of Normanville, but the feeling between them had changed. A few months later, we received the very sad news that Janie had found the 'rocky' parts of their marriage too hard to live with and had taken off for another relationship. Richard, with two small children to care for and a very intense work and travel program, found it necessary to ask the WA Government for a transfer back to Perth to a more home based position. It was very deflating for all of us.

But life at Government House went on at its galloping speed, although Jim and I, on very occasional weekends, were able to escape the formalities of this unusual 'gold-fish bowl' life and drive, on our own, down to our beloved 'Block' on the Blackmore River. There we could enjoy a brief couple of days of normality with the dust and the campfire, kerosene lanterns and skinny dips in the warm river, long intimate chats by the camp-fire, and luxurious sleeps on mattresses in the fly-wire donga that protected us from the mosquitoes and *'things that go bump in the night'*. Chattering corollas in the trees and a misty morning sun would wake us to a beautiful day of peace and quiet, with Jim cooking breakfast over the wood fire. These trips were made even better for me by the fact that the staff packed up the Government House truck for us; we had huge eskies containing all the food and drink that we could possibly need for these brief getaways, along with sheets and towels and a supply of candles and matches, whiskey, brandy and wine. And, of course, all this got cleaned up by the staff once we returned to the comforts of the House. It was a blissful respite.

But time moved on, and Jim was becoming weary of the very public life that he was leading. His health became a bit fragile; first he had an arthroscopy done on a painful knee that had been bothering him for some time. This was followed by a sharp attack of shingles, fortunately quickly arrested by a very astute local doctor. But then he was laid low by a very nasty development of *polymyalgia rheumatica*, or 'inflammation of many muscles'. Both of these were very painful and exhausting conditions and this led him to decide that he did not want to continue for much longer in this very demanding position of Administrator of the Northern Territory. Three and a half years was almost twice the length of time that he had originally said he would do the job for.

So it was agreed that we would leave Government House, and the Northern Territory on December 4th 1992.

On December 3rd, my 66th birthday, we gathered all the staff in the big formal dining room. With its long cedar table that had seated twenty four illustrious guests at various dinner parties, the large painting by Marie Tuck (a South Australian forbear of mine) that hung over the long cedar sideboard, and the elaborate crystal chandelier, it was the most handsome room in the House. The staff, all twenty of them, looked a little nervous and not sure what was expected of them, when Jim wheeled in a traymobile laden with colourfully wrapped presents. I am sure that they thought that this was a big show for my birthday. But Jim quickly made it clear that the gifts were for the staff, each one chosen carefully by us both. We hoped the gifts would be a small reminder of the time that we had spent with them, and a small appreciation of all that they had done for us in the past three and a half years.

The next day, it was a warm but sad farewell. Jim was presented with the three flags—the Australian flag, the Northern Territory flag and the Aboriginal flag—that had flown on our flagpole during Jim's residency, and the Chef, Diane, had given me an enormous, beautifully iced Christmas cake that she had made for us to take to share with the Perth families.

And finally we were driven in NT1 by Brian, our faithful, always punctual, and sometimes irksomely meticulous chauffeur, around the wide circular drive at the front of this historic old house, and waved off by our loyal friends, the staff from the House and from the Office, and out through the white picket gates for the last time.

RETIREMENT FOR REAL

And now we were back to the quiet, domesticity of suburban life in our red brick house in Cottesloe. And it was surprisingly pleasant to sit quietly on our back lawn, with a whiskey and a brandy, Jim with his cigarette or two, surrounded by our own small garden, and preparing our own simple meal.

So now what to do next?

We were very happy to be available to help Richard with Little Tim and Hannah. They had returned from England and were sorting out their lives with an *au pair* in place of a mother, and the two young ones were settling into the local North Cottesloe Primary School, so we had plenty of time to spend with these two delightful young grandchildren and to become more involved in their lives.

Jim was given a small but quite interesting job chairing a National committee of inquiry for the Department of Veteran's Affairs. He was also a selector for Awards that resulted from the three year Government initiative of recognition of the pressing need for Reconciliation and acknowledgement of the existence, *and* the achievements, of the Aboriginal people and communities in this country. These two 'jobs' gave him the opportunity to still be in touch with communities across Australia, and to travel occasionally to other States.

But it still left us plenty of time to enjoy the beautiful weather of Perth, to swim at its lovely white beaches, to walk in King's Park, and to visit our delicious little house at Gracetown. I had continued my interest in the YWCA of Perth and as well as being on the Board of Directors I chaired a Committee that oversaw the programs that the Perth 'Y' was conducting in the community.

Jim was now 68 and I was 67 so we still had quite a bit of energy and enthusiasm for travel, but this time within Australia. So we packed our four-wheel drive Holden Jackaroo and set off for Darwin. We were both a little apprehensive at the thought of spending two weeks, just the two of us, passing through the wide open empty spaces of the 4,000 kilometres that stretch between Perth and Darwin. We need not have worried. These were, I think, the happiest times of our whole marriage, so that, as we approached Darwin, much as we were excited to be seeing our beloved three grandchildren and their parents, when we were about to turn left onto the Stuart Highway, we each murmured, a little guiltily,

"Shall we just turn south at Katherine and keep going?"

We did three of these wonderful open road trips. Each time we came home a different way. Each time we saw new and wonderful scenes and met new and fascinating characters. Each time we revelled in the simplicity of our way of life, staying in remote road houses or little cabins in caravan parks, stopping, roadside, for a coffee (and the essential cigarette for the driver), at some remote and absolutely quiet, empty patch of Australian beauty. We seemed to agree about everything, discussing so many aspects of our nearly fifty years of marriage together. It had been a long journey, and not without its problems. But now, with all four children settled reasonably happily in their independent lives; and with our six, soon to be seven, beautiful and healthy grandchildren, we could start to understand a little of what our life had all been about, and even perhaps to appreciate a little of what we had achieved together. This was, most certainly, the most precious time of our life together. How lucky we had been.

And number seven grandchild arrived safely on 6th December 1993. James Nicholas Muirhead, born to Sue Clear and Tim, was a very cuddly little roly-poly baby boy with chubby cheeks just like his father had had. As we were much more available in Perth for baby-sitting than we had been with the other grandchildren, Jim and I were able to enjoy a little more of Jamie's early years. A delightful moment was always soon after six-thirty in the evening, when, after dinner and bath, he would quietly move up to my knee and say:

"Bottle-n-bed?"

And that would be Jamie finished for the day.

Then five years later, Jim's yearning for another little girl in the family was fulfilled when Feathers, (Jane Featherstone), Richard's new English wife, gave birth to a delicious little baby girl, on 27th August 1998. Originally named Katherine Elizabeth Muirhead, (although Richard had hoped he could call her Ocean), this fair haired, blue-eyed little treasure became Kitty and then Kit, both names recalling her paternal great-grandmother, Jim's Mother, who was always called Kit or Kitty.

So, five little boys and three little girls made a delightful collection of grandchildren to add to the enjoyment of our lives together. And again we had the time, and the delight, of being able to have them stay with us for visits and become a very important part of our lives.

We were also able to do one more overseas trip. This one was in an organised group, which seemed to lessen the anxiety that Jim always felt when he was out of the security of his own country, and it was a trip of his choice and his planning. He arranged that we would join a tour managed by the Australian War Memorial, travelling to Gallipoli for Anzac Day, and then on to the battlefields of World War One in France and Belgium where his father had seen action. It didn't really appeal to me much, as I had always been a bit of an ostrich where war, or death or anything at all unpleasant was concerned, having the escapist attitude that, *if I shut my eyes it won't be happening.*

However, of course I agreed to the trip and, of course, it was an amazingly wonderful experience. Tragic and moving most certainly, but so informative, educational and heart-warming in many ways, particularly in the strong connection that the people of Turkey showed to us as Australians, even though our forefathers had tried, drastically unsuccessfully, to invade their country. This attitude of the Turks that we met seemed to be encapsulated in the beautiful words of Mustafa Kemal Ataturk, who was the Turkish leader at the time of this War, that are inscribed in Anzac Cove:

> *'Those heroes that shed their blood and lost their lives,*
> *You are now lying in the soil of a friendly country.*
> *Therefore, rest in peace.*
> *There is no difference between the Johnnies and the Mehmets*
> *to us where they lie side by side here in this country of ours.*
> *You, the mothers who sent your sons from far away countries,*
> *Wipe away your tears; your sons are now lying in our bosom*
> *and are in peace. After having lost their lives on this land*
> *they have become our sons as well.'*

SECTION 7
AND THEN...

AND THEN...

And then he died!!

With very little warning and in the middle of the night, in Darwin, he died!!

This man who had shaped my life into what it had become, who had provided me with my reason for existence, our four children, and now our eight beloved and fascinating grandchildren, just died. Lying beside me, at Bill and Margie's house at London Road, Coolalinga, worrying a little about the Mary River Houseboat trip we were doing with the family for the next couple of days, on Tuesday, July 20, 1999, at 1.30 in the morning, James Henry Muirhead drew four long shuddering breaths, and wordlessly, and painlessly, left me forever.

Jim had been a little restless during the night, feeling slightly nauseous and sweaty. I offered to take him up to the Royal Darwin Hospital, but he just said, 'don't be silly,' and, hoping to help him settle, I shared a Valium tablet with him. I slept for a little bit, but woke at about 1.00 am and he was sitting up on the edge of the bed.

"Are you okay, honey?"

I sat up beside him and put my hand on his shoulder, but, without a word, he fell back on the bed, quite rigid, and just stopped breathing. I quickly called Bill, who was in the room almost at once. He had been aware of the restlessness of our bathroom light going on and off throughout the first part of the night as Jim made urgent visits to the toilet.

Immediately, Bill moved skilfully into CPR. He seemed to know exactly what to do. And within about ten minutes, at the prompt summons of Margie, and guided by her torch light at the gate to show the way, the St John's Ambulance crew was there with all the equipment to bring a person back to life. They put his body on the floor to provide a firmer surface for the CPR and shock treatment machine, but as I sat on the floor, holding Jim's bare foot, I felt like saying to them:

"There's no-one in there. Don't worry. Jim has just left his body. He's not coming back."

The St John's men took Jim into their ambulance, saying to me,

"No. You come separately. We have things to do," and Bill quickly brought his car to the front door and bundled me into it, holding my hand firmly, all the long 30 kilometre drive up to the Darwin Hospital. We didn't say much. We were both a bit numb, I guess. But at one stage Bill suddenly said, quite grumpily,

"Well, if you didn't want to come on the Mary River house boats why didn't you just say so!"

"Who are you talking to?" I asked him.

"To Dad. He's sitting on the back seat."

And maybe some part of him was.

On the way up to the hospital I rang Janet to tell her that Dad had had a massive heart attack and we were heading for the Hospital. Amazingly, by the time we arrived, she and Nick and a tearful Joshua were waiting for us. We were a very subdued little group as we waited in the gloomy hallway outside the Emergency room at the Hospital. But it was not long before the doctor called me into his office and told me that they could not revive Jim. He had died. But I already knew that. He was somewhere nearby, but he certainly wasn't in his tired old body.

We all went back to Janet and Nick's house and Nick gave me a huge neat brandy. I think I drank it. But I also insisted on ringing first Richard and then Tim, both in Perth. Fairly brief words to each of them... just the facts. Their father had had a massive heart attack and was no longer alive. I still felt quite numb and a bit unreal. Then Bill drove me home to his house. Margie and little eight year old Julia met me on the veranda. *Then* I sobbed in Margie's arms and she led me back to my bed, a bed which was to be empty for the rest of my life.

Then everything happened so quickly. By lunchtime later that day Richard and Tim had arrived from Perth. How did they do that? A magic carpet, or just amazing organisation. The Coroner said that there must be an autopsy!! But no, Richard fixed it that Jim's GP in Perth, a mate of his, gave the authority that a specialist had detected a *'glitch in the electric wiring around the heart,'* and so no autopsy. The Territory Government wanted to give Jim a State Funeral. The boys and Janet said, "Okay, as long as we have a say in it and it isn't too stuffy."

Arrangements were made, and the rest of the family, Feathers and Sue and the five Perth grandchildren arrived together on the Thursday. So here they all were, an additional ten people to be bedded, and fed, at Bill and Margie's house. And without any fuss, it seemed, it was all just *done*. I felt so safe and *cared for*, and I was softly cushioned by the gentle presence of all these so familiar and much loved young people, my family, who seemed to know exactly what needed to be done, when I needed some company and when I needed to be on my own.

An especially wonderful thing happened on the afternoon that all the family went in to Darwin to say their farewells to their father and grandfather. I rested in my room, sometimes dozing a little, while they were away. At times I heard small noises in the kitchen, but thought little of it. When the family returned from their sad visit, they found every kitchen bench was covered with plates, pots and tins of home made soups, stews, cakes, puddings, and even a bowl of sieved vegetables for the eight month old

Kit. Bill's amazing neighbour, Bev, with two small children of her own, had baked and cooked all day to provide this abundance of prepared food to help Bill's family cope with their shock and grief. Quietly she had left this most generous and practical statement of her sympathy and support. A wonderful young woman.

When they all came home from seeing Jim for the last time, young six year old Jamie came onto my bed. He lay beside me and quietly and thoughtfully said,

"I saw a rabbit once that had died, and it just lay there not moving. And Gramps was just lying there and he wasn't moving."

That was all. We held hands and just stayed quietly together until he heard some interesting noises in the garden and hopped up to join his older cousins on the four-wheeled lawn mower and the train of small trailers that Bill had set up for them all to tow each other around his bush covered five-acre block.

I later learned that thirteen year old Jesse had stuck a two dollar coin onto a card with *'Buy yourself an ice-cream, Gramps,'* written on it, and had tucked it in the pocket of Jim's shirt. Gramps used to often post off a card like this to the grandkids when we were away, so Jesse was just returning the gift. Nick left a miniature bottle of whiskey and half a packet of cigarettes in Jim's pocket, and Janet had taken a lock of her father's hair, and left him a lock of hers, and Richard left the maps of the marathon motorbike ride he and his girlfriend, Janet Lockie, had done together from London to Malaysia many years before.

And so they all grieved in their own quiet and private way. And at times it felt that I was grieving more for all these young people who had lost an adored father and grandfather, than I did for myself.

It was an extraordinary week. All four kids each instinctively took on the role that suited them best. Janet became the hostess, making sure that the interstate and overseas relatives and friends who came to Darwin were met and taken to their accommodation, and arranging an evening at the Sailing Club so that they could meet all the family. Richard took on any business arrangements that needed to be attended to. Tim organised the ritual, cultural and more spiritual side of things, checking that the readings from the Bible had meaning for Dad and not just 'rewards in Heaven' sort of stuff. He found the right Larrakia elder, Bill Risk, to give a welcome to Country, which this fine and respected Aboriginal man extended to a most respectful acknowledgement of Jim as a 'very important lawman to the Aboriginal people'. And, unexpectedly, but as a great honour, the local Larrakia people performed a special corroboree under a white flowered frangipani tree outside the Cathedral. Bill Risk also gave his authority to fly the Aboriginal Flag at half-mast at the Cathedral after Harold Thomas, the designer of the flag, had reminded Tim, via a colleague, that the flag could only be flown with the authority of Aboriginal people.

Bill said, "This is my land. You will fly the Flag."

Added to all that, Tim wrote and delivered a warm, personal and sometimes amusing, eulogy. And Bill (son Bill) did the fix-it jobs, found things for all the children to do, and re-arranged his house to accommodate the 200% increase in its occupants.

A Government protocol officer, and the Anglican priest, came to Bill and Margie's home to make all the official arrangements for the funeral which was to be held in Christchurch Cathedral on Saturday July 24 1999. The two men were very respectful and careful in broaching each part of the arrangements. What the boys should wear at the funeral caused a minor skirmish.

"We'll wear short sleeved shirts, nice colourful ones," said Tim. "Probably Dad will too. He loved the casualness of the Territory."

"Your father will be dressed in long-sleeved *white* shirt and tie," said the protocol officer firmly. "And so will all you men."

"Oh no." Tim replied. "It suits us all better to look bright and colourful."

Peter, the protocol officer, looked a bit grim and said again,

"You *will* wear long sleeved white shirts and ties. This is a State occasion. Your father was a respected and important man here in the Territory. It will be long sleeved white shirts and ties."

"Oh," said Tim, and the other boys looked deflated but resignedly accepted this fact.

Then the protocol officer said:

"And how many limousines will you need to take the family to the service?"

"NO!" said Richard, "no limousines."

"But of course you are entitled to limousines. How many should I order?"

"We don't want limousines," said Richard. "We won't be separated into different cars. We will all travel together. We will travel in a bus. Give me some names and I will organise it."

"Oh. Um." said the poor protocol officer. "Let me see. A bus, eh? Well there is one that I know. Let me see, here is the number. It's called *Jim's Luxury Tours.*"

The boys and Janet looked at each other, the little priest's eyebrow went up near his hair line, the protocol officer looked vaguely surprised, then quite shocked and embarrassed, and suddenly everyone was collapsing in helpless laughter. It was a surprisingly precious moment.

And so it all happened, as these things seem to do. People, tears, hugs, handshakes. A huge crowd at the Cathedral, including Judges, Lawyers, the Chief Minister, the Administrator and many, many friends and acquaintances from our 15 wonderful years in this remote, strange and special part of the country. There was a large reception provided by the Northern Territory Government, and later, a gathering at Janet and Nick's house in Ludmilla, somehow drawn together and organised by Janet and her friends and some of Margie's family.

In between these two gatherings was another quiet, but special, moment. Just the immediate family, seventeen of us, followed the hearse in our oddly named bus, out to the Crematorium where a very simple service was held by the priest. I sat in the front pew of the tiny little chapel, with grandchildren on either side of me, and found little Kitty tugging at my skirt as she crawled from the row behind us and under my seat. Then just before the curtains were to close on the coffin that contained my husband of forty-nine and a half years, something stirred in me and I quickly moved forward and placed both my hands on the casket, feeling the strength of that strange and final farewell. And at once, all the grandchildren were gathered around me and placing their hands with mine. Such a flow of love went with this one man as he was taken from us for the very last time.

How my sons and daughter, my daughters-in-law, son-in-law and my beloved grandchildren closed in around me during that strange period following the funeral. The love and support of all these young people, their care and their sadness flowed over and around me, enveloping me in a warm and most tender embrace. Not many words were spoken, but so many, many tiny actions, small attentions, thoughtful arrangements and funny, unexpected, gentle jokes and laughter kept me from being totally overwhelmed and lost at this sudden gap that had thrown me into widowhood.

I stayed with Bill and Margie for a month after Jim's death. They assured me that I need *never* go home if that was what I wanted, and I felt they really meant it. It was a quiet time. A few friends visited, but I preferred to just be with the family or rather pensively on my own.

Bill, Margie and I went to Alice Springs where the lawyers of Central Australia had a small gathering to honour, with affection and gently humorous memories, their much loved and respected past Judge. Then Bill and I flew on to Adelaide where we met with Janet, Richard and Tim. After putting Jim's ashes in the family plot, with his parents and grandparents and other relatives at North Road Cemetery, we hosted a Memorial Service in St Andrews Church in Walkerville. This Church was where Jim and I had been married and our four children christened, and where many other family ceremonies had been held over the past 70 or 80 years. An overflowing Church of people was followed by *another* gathering of friends and dozens of relatives in the local Hotel, organised again by a special friend of Janet's, who was also a distant relative of mine, Myranwy Kaines. Here Richard kept an eye on proceedings and particularly the Bar outgoings, so when he came up to me and said, 'Some of our mates would like a whiskey in memory of Dad,' of course I said 'yes' even though he added, a little sheepishly, 'we *have* hit the 1K'. But it seemed to be a noisy, jolly gathering, and Jim would have *loved* it.

I went back to Darwin with Bill, and stayed with him and Margie, Chris and Julia for a few more days. Finally, I knew I must return to Perth and take up my new, and probably challenging, life in our Cottesloe home.

Of course, the Perth family were all in the house to meet me, and again it felt that they were protecting me from the shock of an empty house. And Hannah stayed the first couple of nights with me to break the emptiness.

And then there was yet *another* gathering, *'for our Perth mates and your friends who want to say goodbye to Dad, too,'* said the two boys. I wasn't too enthusiastic, but the boys organised everything. People were kind, warm, and generous in their attention to me. A

little to my surprise I found that the fact that all these people—
the new friends that we had found in Perth and the many
younger friends of the boys—had taken the trouble to come to
this gathering, gave me a positive and very warm feeling that I
really had 'come home'.

There were several short speeches and tributes at this gathering,
and young Tim, not quite nineteen, read his few words to his
beloved Gramps. He had dressed in a tight fitting pink shirt and
baggy shorts that he found amongst Gramps' clothes and topped
it off with a battered old cloth hat, taking a gentle swing at his
grandfather's *style and high sense of fashion*. His words were quite
light-hearted and factual: Gramps' super punctuality; getting all
the grandkids names muddled, so usually settling for 'Boy,' and
always muddling Janet and Hannah. But at the last paragraph
Tim gave a small gulp and turned away quietly sobbing. Richard,
his Dad, who had been standing close by, took the paper from his
hands saying, "not sure if I can do this either," but, taking a deep
breath he read out these words:

> *"Gramps loved Cowaramup Bay and the house at Gracetown,*
> *and going there with him and Granny was always fun. When*
> *other people think of going away with their grandfather many*
> *would groan, but I would jump at the opportunity. Gramps*
> *particularly loved whale sightings and this is what my last*
> *few words to Gramps were about.*
>
> *Over the phone to him in Darwin, me at home after a week*
> *down south:*
> *"I saw some whales down south Gramps"*
> *"Wow, Boy, big ones?"*
> *"Yeah, and in pretty close too."*
> *"Whacko… Well, 'bye Boy."*
> *"Bye Gramps"…*
>
> > *"Bye Gramps"*

THE YEARS AFTER

'*So what happens now?*' I wondered to myself.

It was strangely comforting to be back in the home that Jim and I had created and shared over the past fourteen years. Jim's presence was certainly to be felt in many corners of it: sitting in his armchair close by the fireplace; out on the back verandah, with cigarette and whiskey in hand, and gazing out on his lovey colourful garden; snoring quietly and contentedly on his side of the bed.

Strangely, on my first day home on my own, a small bird sat on the ledge outside the kitchen window, just hopping a little and tapping on the window, and it stayed there for quite a few minutes. I have never seen one do this, before or after. Was this a special visitor or messenger?

But the hardest time of the day, I found, was the last thing at night. After reading myself almost to sleep, turning off the light, and knowing that there was a big empty space beside me, and then being fully awake again to the knowledge that this would never change, is something that still, seventeen years on, keeps me restless and awake far longer than I care to be.

But always, the kids and grandkids were just *there*. Richard would drop in for brief visits, do a few fix-it jobs, and breeze off. Feathers would drop by for a cuppa, or drop little 12 month old Kitty off, asking me if I could just watch her for a bit while she, Feathers, did a bit of shopping. It made me feel useful, and gave me the joy of watching this serious little girl select plastic basins to put on her head, or interact gently with the fluffy tail of our placid old Border Collie, Bonnie. Young Hannah asked me to teach her to play the piano and we had some happy and frustrating struggles with that challenging instrument. Tim would come down from Leederville when he could and sit on the back decking with me and have long, leisurely chats, making himself so available for any problems I may want to discuss. My doctor had asked me if I needed 'grief counselling'. I said 'no,' not adding that I didn't need it. I had Tim. Janet and Bill rang often from Darwin and kept me in touch with anything that was happening there. They each had me to stay with them for two or three weeks at a time, including me in their lives and in their families, and ensuring that I could be part of the Darwin life-style again, including camping trips, drinks around the pool with young friends and sunset picnics. And Janet took the time to shepherd me on several overseas trips, taking me to beautiful and remote corners of Bali where I could see the traditional cultural side of the Balinese people. Once again she was widening my world by helping me to discover new experiences. And together we had fun, and lots of laughter. My daughter became a very special friend to me. Ours has been a really important relationship that I have cherished so much over these past seventeen years.

And the older grandkids, of course, were always somewhere around, and full of bounce and joy. They all made sure that I didn't have too much time to feel the loneliness.

Jim's garden gave me plenty to do too. At first I felt duty-bound to try and keep it alive just for Jim's sake. He had enjoyed it so much. Then I found that I really enjoyed the activity and the exercise, and the satisfaction of seeing something flower and flourish. And when Tim said one day, "You know, I think the garden looks better now than when Dad was doing it," I felt a little surge of pride and achievement.

But those first months were a sombre time for me. There was a strange emptiness in my life, and I slowly realised that it really was up to me to try and close over that gaping space. I found great comfort in going to our little house in Gracetown, often just on my own, though always with the dog and the cat, of course. It was a time for reflective melancholy, for good memories, and for self-searching thoughts of what had been, and '*what to do now.*' At Gracetown I could be busy and occupied, but not have to worry about other people. I found it very healing, and quite comforting to be in a place that Jim and I had shared so happily for fifteen years. His presence was very much there, and it was good.

Back in Perth I had a very special friend, a woman whom I had met over the Bridge table during the lessons that I went to when we first moved to Perth. Her name was Ros Wales. She was 13 years older than me, but had more energy and enthusiasm for life than I could ever imagine having. She was open and cheerful, and hated negative thoughts and actions, especially sickness and death. And yet, when I first came back to Perth after Jim died, she called to see me, sat down with her cup of tea and said:

"Now, do you feel like talking about it?"

And all of a sudden, I did. And poor Ros got the lot, right from the very first moments that Jim started to be stressed and restless on the night of the 19th July 1999, all the way through to the last tears on the day of the funeral.

But she listened well and attentively, and I felt oh so much better after just recalling it all out loud. Ros became my closest Perth friend, and also my role model, and I owe her so much for just helping me to find my way towards an independent, productive and satisfying single life.

Another positive influence for me was a woman whose name I don't even know. I remember very little of the rather large reception that the Northern Territory Government held straight after the Service for Jim's funeral. But a comment from this unknown person stayed with me loud and clear. She said to me,

"When my father died, my mother didn't bother with proper meals, and she became really quite ill."

That was all, but I stored it away, and reflected on it, and have always made sure to cook and eat regular and balanced meals at all times. I actually managed to lose eight kilograms of my bulgy weight as I abandoned the sausage roll and sticky bun lunches that were Jim's favourites, and the sausages and mash, and pudding and cream that we nearly always had for dinner. And I guess I gradually felt altogether better for it.

Chrissie Streitberg, a younger woman who was a friend of Richard and Feathers, very firmly and persuasively invited me to be her Bridge partner, playing at the Bridge Club on the one day when all the serious players were there. It was a challenge for me, but a good one, and her patience and cheerful encouragement of my mediocre standard of play helped me to build a little more confidence in my ability to do something on my own.

Both the Perth sons, their wives and their friends were generous in their inclusion of me in so many of their activities. I was grateful for every invitation that came my way, and tried to make sure that I wasn't a drag to have around. And the whole family gathered in Perth for our first Christmas 'without Dad', and to spend New Year's Eve at a little hotel in Fremantle to welcome in the New Millennium.

So I was surviving, and, with loving support all around me, I was managing it more or less on my own. I was learning to say 'me' and 'mine' and 'I', instead of 'us' and 'ours' and 'we'. I was coping with the business affairs of running a home and garden, a holiday house and its maintenance, insurance, finances and snippets of social life. I was fortunate to have a quite generous income from Jim's Judicial Pension, although at first the reduction by one third of the amount that he had been receiving since his retirement, came as a bit of a nasty surprise, and I drew up a budget to see where it all seemed to be going. Bill helped me to select and buy a smaller car, and Richard was invaluable in keeping the Gracetown house in good repair. But I had no wish to travel, not even back to Darwin at this stage, and whenever I went out to a game of Bridge or a morning tea, I took the quickest route home as soon as I could, and didn't really relax until I was back in that familiar security of the home in Cottesloe where I still felt Jim's spirit hovering comfortably.

Then, when I reached the unlikely age of 73, an old, slightly tantalising, connection was rekindled.

It was almost a year after Jim had died so unexpectedly, and I was slowly coming to terms with the process of grieving, of living alone, and of being surrounded by the memories of the ups and downs, the successes and the short-comings of the long relationship, spanning more than fifty years, that Jim and I had had.

One evening sometime in June I drove home from Richard and Feathers' house after a cheerful and noisy dinner with them and with Little Tim, Hannah and young Kitty. The answering machine was blinking at me, and as I played it back, there was a belated message of sympathy from someone in Adelaide. I played it back a couple of times, just to be sure, hardly believing that it was that deep, well-modulated voice that I hadn't heard for more than thirty years, way back in the Adelaide days.

"Well," said I to Bonnie the dog. "Fancy that. I wonder how he knew?"

And memories came flooding back to me, disturbing my peaceful night in an extraordinary and most unbecoming way, particularly for a septuagenarian!!

The next morning, the phone rang again... and yes... it was that voice again.

Most suitable and genuine expressions of sympathy and concern were made to me. And then, casually...

"Are you likely to be in Adelaide anytime this year?"

Now, just a little breathless and feeling a bit unreal, I replied that as I had decided to go to Darwin at last and was heading there in the next month, I could, maybe, drop off in Adelaide for a couple of days, and meet up just for a drink or something.

And in this New Millennium of the year 2000 that is what I did.

This unexpected reunion seemed to appeal to both of us, and we met in this way a couple of times a year for the next three and a half years. Neither of us wanted to disturb our families with any weird ideas, so it was much simpler to discuss our arrangement with absolutely no-one. But it certainly brought a new spring into my step, and also, perhaps, a growing faith in myself as an independent woman. And it was stimulating and fun, and completely away and beyond the reality of my daily world. Another step, perhaps, in my rehabilitation, for which I will always be grateful. I was much nearer to becoming a person in my own right, with a knowledge of my ability to make my own choices and my own decisions. It was a liberating experience, and I was aware of my spirit enjoying this feeling of freedom. And also, I guess, a smidgin of pride that there was still something about me that was a little bit attractive to at least one person.

Unfortunately, about this time, Tim's marriage to Sue finally came to an unhappy ending, and Tim and the boys moved in with me while everyone was sorting themselves out and getting used to all the new circumstances that they had to cope with. This was a sad blow to us all, and it was not made any easier for me by not having Jim to lean on or turn to for his wise advice, which he was always able to produce when really serious things happened in the family. But it was good to know that I could be useful when someone in the family needed some help.

After both these things settled down, I knew that I needed a further occupation, particularly on the weekends. I couldn't expect my Perth family to always be keeping an eye on me on Saturdays and Sundays, which were their busy times with their own children. So I launched into Croquet. And I *loved* it. The people were very friendly, the game was interesting, challenging and fun, and the exercise, concentration and fresh air were just what I needed to give me a new passion. It was definitely another step in the right direction. Life after the end of a marriage was becoming manageable after all. And I started to travel a bit too. I joined a couple of groups that toured Europe, following the Australian Chamber Orchestra on their Continental tour, and seeing wonderful and interesting parts of many of those ancient towns that we passed through. I also took a couple of cruises from Fremantle, one to Bali, and one to Mauritius, and then on to Cape Town to stay with Sue Handley (Ross), one of my 'best friends' from my school days. Again, I 'managed' on my own, making friends as I went along, surprising myself at the ease with which I struck up conversations with complete strangers, but appreciating that that was one of the valuable skills that I had learned from my special friend, Ros Wales.

AND ONE MORE

A particularly wonderful addition, and a bit of a surprise to everyone, occurred in the year 2000. Bill claimed that it was a special gift from Dad.

On 13 August 2000, with the help and support of Chris, Julia and Bill, (with Chris, at the age of 13 actually cutting the cord!) Margie gave birth to a delicious little baby girl, Katherine Jean. She was an absolute joy. Bill was convinced that *'Dad had picked her out especially*' and sent her along to help fill the huge gap that had been left by his death. Of all the grandchildren, Katie was the only one who looked at all like me, and that similarity continued in a quite uncanny way for several years. Later, she became much more like her sister, Julia, in her appearance; a much better outcome, I thought. But in those early years I found it fascinating to watch this small replica of me, wandering off independently across the wide lawns on Bill and Margie's property at Coolalinga, and growling "Do 'way, doggie," when the large Razor-back dogs wanted to play with this little brown bundle of a baby girl, clad only in a nappy.

But a couple of years later Katie's big sister, Julia, gave us all a horrible fright when she was just 13 years old. She developed a horrendous headache, which the staff at the Darwin Hospital could not work out how to manage, and so immediately sent her off 'down South' for specialised attention. She arrived in Perth, in a wheelchair, with her mother, Margie, her lovely gentle Nanna, (Margie's Mum, Julie) and the little two and a half year old sister. The doctors at Princess Margaret Hospital discovered that Julia had had a brain haemorrhage, and there was little they could do but watch and wait. And that is what Margie did too, not leaving the hospital, or Julia's bed, day or night, while she watched her daughter suffer the searing pain of the pressure of the haemorrhage on her brain. Fortunately the bleed was *between* the ventricles instead of *into* the brain which could have had ghastly results, but it was still a very tense time for us all. Very soon Bill came down from Darwin to be of support to Margie, leaving Chris in the care of one of Margie's sisters.

Margie's Mum, Julie, did a wonderful job of keeping Katie happy and gently occupied while her parents spent all their time at the hospital. They all stayed with me in Cottesloe while Julia had CAT scans, MRI's, angiograms, and finally, stereotactic radiotherapy which involved encasing the patient's head in a steel frame and directing the radiotherapy beams *directly* and specifically at the tiny AVM (arterio-venous malformation) that had caused this fearsome bleed. Unfortunately, by a miscalculation of the thickness of Julia's 13 year old skull, the beams misfired. Thankfully they didn't cause any further damage, but they completely failed to destroy the malformation. However, after seven weeks of hospitalisation and treatment, and a slight distortion of Julia's eyesight, which we were assured would improve, as it eventually did, it was decided that Julia and her family could return to Darwin. It had been a dramatic and worrying time in all our lives.

And so, between my very special family, Bridge, Croquet, the theatre, Ros and a few other special friends and acquaintances, my life settled more or less calmly into the single existence of a very fortunate, reasonably healthy, financially secure, relatively happy, widowhood. Visitors—mostly relatives—came and stayed, and I had good opportunities of connecting and spending more time with cousins and nieces of my own family. My cousin Marie was a regular visitor, and I often stayed with her in Adelaide. The house at Gracetown became a haven of peace and re-vitalisation. I acquired a small, cuddly tri-colour Cocker Spaniel pup called Sam, who was my dearest companion for nearly 13 years. My grey tabby much-travelled cat, Maisie, finally, in her twentieth year, breathed her last quiet breath, wrapped in a towel on my dining-room table, me holding her paw and stroking her gently on her way. Much later, an exquisite tortoise-shell kitten called Google delighted me for a year before she turned into a beastly scratchy, bitey teen-ager, which she is now, gradually, outgrowing.

We had many 'whole family' gatherings over the years for various celebrations: Christmas, both in Perth and at Gracetown, the New Millennium on the beach at Cottesloe, Richard's 50th birthday at Cape Levique, Rottnest holidays, and a major trip to Italy, including sailing through the islands of Croatia. Surprisingly, everyone in the family made the effort to be at these gatherings, and, on the whole they were harmonious and fun despite the inevitable tensions and misunderstandings that can arise in the chaos and confusion of twenty-four very different people, thrown together for an extended period.

My eightieth birthday, in the year 2006, was quite a celebration. The family took over, and with a minimum of input from me, they arranged a wonderful gathering of about 90 people of all ages on our, no *my*, back lawn. The guests were summoned by an amazing invitation designed and created by Margie, in which somehow I was shown as the Queen in all her regalia, crown and all. It was a happy and relaxed gathering, with face-painting a highlight. Wonderful creations emerged, including a fried egg on a balding head, and all the middle-aged friends of my kids jostled for position as to '*who could go next*!!!' The artistic results were magnificent.

There were speeches of course. Lots of nice things were said. A couple of friends spoke kindly. Then Janet spoke, with lovely daughterly words, forgetting all those miserable times that I let her down in so many ways, and highlighting the positives as she saw them. Hannah, with amazing confidence at 23, spoke of *her* learning from her grandmother, 'about gambling, drugs and sex'!! Fortunately I don't remember the details of her slightly over-the-top stories. And then Richard took the microphone and told the '*real* story of his *real* mother', and all the home truths of his childhood came out, every one of them piercingly accurate. There was a lot of hilarity at my embarrassment.

Jamie who must have been about twelve, and reading out his own words announced that:

> *"...I thought to myself, 'does Granny know how I feel about her?'...*
> *"My granny is one of the most important people to me on the face of this earth...'*

He went on to mention the things he had learnt from me, and:

> *'Her favourite saying is 'OH MY HAT!!!'..."*

And then,

> *"I'll never forget the time when we were camping. It was pouring down rain and Dad had one of his common migraines. Granny squeezed us all into her one little tent and we played games aaaaallll day."...*

...though he failed to mention that Katie, aged about thirteen months, had a rich nappy-full of last night's dinner which, of course, we couldn't escape to change; and yet not one of the kids complained!!!

Then he added,

> *"..she gives us hugs whenever we ask. With four children, nine grandchildren and one great-grandchild, you'd think she'd run out of love, but oooohhh no. She's still dishing up as much love as she was decades ago, and all evenly too..."*

And he finished with,

> *"So I thank you Granny for teaching me to make pancakes, to play card games, to swim and to almost fold sheets; for your old 1940's sayings, sneaking me choccies, kicking the footy and giving me all the love and compassion I could possibly ask for. I hope you have a wonderful 80th birthday."*

And it was a wonderful birthday.

And on the whole, each gathering was an amazing achievement in organisation and co-operation, careful diplomacy and, I think, a lot of genuine and generous love. The family bond in which Jim had always had such faith, thankfully, still seems to have a strength that can bring us all together, in spite of our many differences. One of the grandchildren recently said, in a note to me,

> *"We have a wonderful bunch of cousins. I'm glad we are all such good mates. A function of the love and leadership we get from the top, and yours and Grampsy's strong love of family,....."*

Jim would have been so proud to hear these words.
But, equally importantly, these bonds are added to by the generous tolerance of those people who have joined the family, either through marriage or close connections, and who are obliged to follow along, and appear to enjoy, these noisy, crazy gatherings as much as most of the family members seem to do. They cannot possibly know how much I appreciate the efforts that they make to ensure that the strength of *family* is given top priority. And even though some of them have moved on to other partnerships, they are still the mothers of some of my grandchildren, they are still important to me and I still enjoy spending time with them and hearing about their lives, and I am grateful that they are willing to still give me some of their time and attention.

And of course, the family keeps growing. Joshua gave me my first great-grandchild, Akaiya, then Tim and Hannah married their long term partners and suddenly there were four more delicious little great-grandchildren, Seb and Mollie, and Bonnie and Joe. And Julia and Glenn, in 2016, added one more cuddly, smiling baby boy, Hamish. And, of course there will be more to come.
And Big Tim at last found his true love in a warm, capable and many-faceted woman, Anne Pickering, who was born and

grew up in Canada, adding a touch of a different culture to bring even more colour and variety into the family. The words of an old music-hall song which I have always loved seem to illustrate the passage of Tim's love life. After talking about the early, but not permanent loves of a young man, the song finishes:

> "...*And it's when he thinks he's past love,*
> *It is then he meets his last love,*
> *And he loves her as he's never loved before.*"

Anne and Tim successfully combined Tim's two boys, Jesse and Jamie, and Anne's son, Mike, into a relatively manageable household, from which each young man has spread his wings to New York, or Melbourne, leaving Tim and Anne to follow their dreams together.

And so the last grand gathering of this wonderful family will be for my 90th birthday late in 2016. And then, I think, my story is complete.

But how strange it is now to look back on my eightieth birthday, and to think back on that evening. At least a dozen of the people who were there on our back lawn are no longer with us. What is this extraordinary passage of Nature that gives some of us the privilege of these extra years that have made my life so totally satisfying and fulfilling, and that have given me this extra time to revel in the friendship, the learning and the love that my beloved grandchildren have bestowed on me.

I look back on special times over the years.

There were occasional precious moments when a grand-child, a very young one, would gaze at me and we would seem to look deep into each other's souls. At such moments I had an overwhelming feeling of connection, of deep communication. This little person seemed to be saying, "I totally trust you. I know you will never let me down." It seemed I was being urged to make a solemn promise. Perhaps that message of trust shaped my total commitment and absorption in each one of these nine special young people who have, each in his or her own way, brought this sense of complete fulfilment into the latter half of my long and very fortunate life.

For there is no doubt, in my mind, that it is my nine grand-children, with all their varying abilities and characters, their generous sharing of their time with me over the past forty years, their different endeavours and achievements, their openness and trust in me, their acceptance of me just as I am, they are the stars of my existence. These are the young people who have contributed to my sense of well-being, even of my personal growth, through the many things that I have learned from them and the special times that I have shared with them, and it is they who have given me a sense of having some useful role to play in my life, even now, in this my tenth decade.

So, becoming a Grandmother has been a long and wonderful journey. I have been given so many opportunities to absorb so much wisdom from so many people throughout my life. Hopefully some of that wisdom, and joy, and love, has filtered through to my beloved grandchildren, and through them, to their children, to help them to make the most of every minute and every opportunity that is granted to them in their lives.

There lie my dreams of the future.

ACKNOWLEDGEMENTS

Writing this memoir has been an interesting 're-living' of my life. I am indebted to a number of people who helped me bring it to fruition…

Without the inspiration and guidance of Rosemary Stevens, who led a short writing course in 2011, I would never have started such a lengthy project. And without son Tim I would never have completed it.

Sue Codee, from Albany, allowed me to use the image of her woodcut, "The Bird and the Key". Then Zoe Beatty, a graphic artist from Darwin, and grandson Joshua, turned that woodcut into the artistic cover.

Daughters-in-law Feathers and Anne, and granddaughter Hannah, worked with Tim to proof-read the manuscript and surprised me with their encouraging, helpful and kind comments.

And Tim… his wisdom, patience, knowledge and enthusiasm have led me, so gently, through to this last page of the indulgence of retracing the steps of these past ninety years.

My sincere thanks to you all.

Ingram Content Group UK Ltd.
Milton Keynes UK
UKHW021816060423
419751UK00014B/441

9 781925 515626